Bao Buns!

Beautiful Bao Bun Recipes
For An Authentic Asian Banquet

1st Edition

By Elise Chen

©Copyright 2018 by Elise Chen. All rights reserved.

This document is geared towards providing exact and reliable information in regards to the topic and issue covered. The publication is sold with the idea that the publisher is not required to render accounting, officially permitted, or otherwise, qualified services. If advice is necessary, legal or professional, a practiced individual in the profession should be ordered.

- From a Declaration of Principles which was accepted and approved equally by a Committee of the American Bar Association and a Committee of Publishers and Associations.

In no way is it legal to reproduce, duplicate, or transmit any part of this document in either electronic means or in printed format. Recording of this publication is strictly prohibited and any storage of this document is not allowed unless with written permission from the publisher. All rights reserved.

The information provided herein is stated to be truthful and consistent, in that any liability, in terms of inattention or otherwise, by any usage or abuse of any policies, processes, or directions contained within is the solitary and utter responsibility of the recipient reader. Under no circumstances will any legal responsibility or blame be held against the publisher for any reparation, damages, or monetary loss due to the information herein, either directly or indirectly.

Respective authors own all copyrights not held by the publisher.

The information herein is offered for informational purposes solely, and is universal as so. The presentation of the information is without contract or any type of guarantee assurance.

Table of Contents

Introduction 1

Chapter 1. Mouthwatering Bao Buns with Pork Filling 3

    Pork Belly Bao Buns with Cucumber and Scallions.. 3

    Shiitake Pork Bao Buns with Sesame Sauce.............. 9

    Barbecue Pork and Pickled Veggie Bao Buns 12

    Bao Buns with Spicy Cider Pork Filling.................. 17

    Braised Pork Belly Bao Buns with Mustard Green and Chili Sauce 22

    Hoisin Ginger Pork Bao Buns with Dressed Slaw... 27

    Pickled Apple and Pork Belly Bao Buns 31

    Pork Bao Buns with Brussels Sprouts...................... 35

Chapter 2. Delectable Bao Buns with Beef Filling...... 39

    Spicy Stir-Fried Beef Bao Buns............................... 39

    Beef Stew Bao Buns with Carrot Pickle 43

    Braised Short Rib Bao Buns with Pickled Vegetables 47

    Beefy Hawaiian Style Bao Buns.............................. 51

    Bulgogi Beef Bao Buns.. 55

Chapter 3. Scrumptious Bao Buns with Chicken/Turkey Filling 57

    Fried Chicken and Milk Gravy Bao Buns.................57

    Gojuchang Chicken Bao Buns with Bahn Mi Slaw..61

    Chicken and Mushroom Bao Buns 65

    Easy Bao Buns with Spicy Chicken Filling..............67

    Black Pepper Turkey Bao Buns................................70

    Bao Buns with Chicken and Chives Stuffing 73

    Turkey and Kimchi Filled Bao Buns 76

    Bao Buns with Curry Fried Chicken Filling.............78

    Teriyaki Turkey Bao Buns..82

    Peking Chicken Bao Buns 83

Chapter 4. Tasty Bao Buns with Fish/Seafood Filling .85

    Spicy Popcorn Shrimp Bao Buns..............................85

    Shrimp Tempura Filled Bao Buns with Sweet and Sour Sauce 88

    Bao Buns with Crispy Fish Fillets 92

    Fish and Crab Bao Buns 96

    Salmon Teriyaki Bao Buns 98

    Chile Butter Lobster Bao Buns...............................101

    Bao Buns Stuffed with Fried Halibut......................103

Chapter 5. Appetizing Bao Buns with Meatless Filling ... 105

- Coconut Filled Bao Buns 105
- Pulled Jackfruit Bao Buns 108
- Bao Buns with Custard Filling 111
- Bao Buns Stuffed with Greens 115
- Easy Red Bean Bao Buns 118
- Shiitake Bok Choy Bao Buns 120
- Breakfast Bao Buns 124
- Tofu Bao Buns with Cucumber Salad 126
- Oyster Mushroom and Seitan Bao Buns 130
- Kimchi Bao Buns 134
- Kimchi and Avocado Mayo Tofu Bao Buns 137
- Orange Sesame Tofu Bao Buns 139

Conclusion 141

Introduction

I want to thank you and congratulate you for purchasing the book, *"Bao Buns! Beautiful Bao Bun Recipes For An Authentic Asian Banquet"*.

This book contains proven steps and strategies for cooking your own downright delicious bao buns – all in their white and soft glory, not to mention their equally enticing fillings.

With bao buns right at your fingertips, you are rest assured of a complete, warm meal or a comforting and hearty snack.

Have fun recreating these recipes with minimal effort, and take pleasure in leaving your family and guests amazed by how you were able to prepare these beautiful bao buns. Prepare to be stunned yourself as you take a bite out of all these best-served-hot bao buns.

Thanks again for choosing this book. I hope you enjoy it!

Chapter 1. Mouthwatering Bao Buns with Pork Filling

Pork Belly Bao Buns with Cucumber and Scallions

Ingredients:

Pork:
Pork belly, boneless, skinless, sliced into quarters (2 ½ pounds)
Sugar (1/2 cup)
Salt, kosher (1/2 cup)
Water, divided (4 ½ cups)
Chicken broth, low sodium (1/2 cup)

Buns:

Milk, dried, nonfat (2 tablespoons)
Yeast, active dry (1/2 teaspoon)
Baking powder (1 ½ teaspoons)
Water, warmed to 115 degrees Fahrenheit, divided (1 cup)
Sugar (3 tablespoons + ¼ teaspoon)
Cake flour (3 ½ cups)
Coconut oil (1 tablespoon + 2 tablespoons) – for greasing & brushing

Accompaniments:

Cucumber, sliced thinly (1 piece)
Scallions, chopped (a handful)
Hoisin sauce (1/4 cup)

Directions:

1. To brine the pork belly:

    a) Fill a small bowl with the water (4 cups), sugar, and salt. Stir until well-combined and the sugar and salt are completely dissolved.

    b) Pour the mixture into a large Ziploc bag. Add the pork belly to the bag, then seal and let sit in a deep dish.

c) Refrigerate and allow the pork to marinate for a minimum of twelve hours.

2. To prepare the bao bun dough:

   a) Fill a small bowl with the warm water (1/4 cup). Add the sugar (a pinch) and yeast, and stir to combine. Let sit for five to ten minutes or until the yeast mixture becomes foamy.

   b) Gradually pour in the remaining warm water (3/4 cup) and dried milk as you whisk continuously.

   c) Meanwhile, fill a medium bowl with the remaining sugar (3 tablespoons) and flour. Stir to combine, and then add the foamy yeast mixture. Use a fork to stir until everything comes into a soft dough.

   d) Knead the dough with clean hands before turning it out onto a surface dusted lightly with flour. Knead again for five minutes or until you have a smooth and elastic dough. Shape into a ball before placing inside a large bowl greased with a little oil. Cover with cling wrap and allow to rise for two hours in a warm spot.

3. To roast the pork belly:

   a) Set the oven at 300 degrees Fahrenheit to preheat. Meanwhile, drain the marinated pork and place at the bottom of an 8x9 baking pan fat side up. Cover with the remaining water (1/2 cup) and broth, then cover the pan with foil. Roast in the oven for two hours and thirty minutes or until extremely tender.

   b) Uncover and turn the oven temperature up to 450 degrees Fahrenheit. Roast for another twenty minutes or until golden on top.

   c) Allow the pork belly to cool on a wire rack for thirty minutes before refrigerating, uncovered, for one hour or until cold.

   d) Slice the cold meat across the grain to form quarter inch portions and return to the baking pan. Allow it to chill, uncovered, for another one hour.

4. To make the bao buns:

   a) Once the dough has doubled in size, knock it down with your fist and place on your flour-dusted work surface. Slightly press with your palm to form a disk before sprinkling the baking powder over its middle part.

b) Gather the dough by the edges and seal in the baking powder by pinching. Sprinkle additional flour on the dough and knead for five minutes or until the baking powder is fully blended in.

c) Place the dough back in the oiled bowl, cover with cling wrap, and let sit for thirty minutes for a second rising.

d) Meanwhile, cut out sixteen pieces of 3x2-inch rectangles from a sheet of wax paper.

e) Once the dough has risen, mold into a sixteen-inch-long roll, form into 16 rounds, dust wall over with a little flour, and cover loosely with cling wrap.

f) After rolling out each dough round into a 6x3-inch oval, lightly brush with oil. Fold each oval dough across the middle without pinching before placing on a wax paper rectangle. Set all buns on a baking sheet, cover with a clean towel, and let stand for thirty minutes for a third rising.

5. To cook the bao buns:

   a) Position a steamer rack inside a wok. Fill the wok with enough water so that one-half-inch of the steamer rack's bottom is covered. Heat to boiling before placing the buns (work with 5 at a time), with their wax papers still on, in the rack. Make sure the buns are evenly spaced before covering and steaming on high for three minutes or until completely cooked and puffy.

   b) Place the cooked bao buns on a plate; after discarding the wax papers, keep warm by covering with a kitchen towel and returning to the steaming skillet.

6. Set the oven at 350 degrees Fahrenheit to preheat, after its rack in the middle. Remove the chilled pork slices from the refrigerator and heat, along with the juices in the baking dish, for about fifteen to twenty minutes or until heated through.

7. Brush the hoisin sauce on each bun's bottom half before topping with 3 slices of pork. Finish by topping with cucumber and scallions. Serve and enjoy.

Shiitake Pork Bao Buns with Sesame Sauce

Ingredients:

Buns:
Salt (1 teaspoon)
White sugar (4 tablespoons)
Baking powder (4 teaspoons)
Water, lukewarm (2 cups)
Yeast (4 teaspoons)
Coconut oil (2 tablespoons)
All-purpose flour (4 cups)

Filling:
Ginger, minced (1 teaspoon)
Sesame oil (1 ½ tablespoons)
Yellow onion, chopped (1/2 piece)
Sugar (1/2 teaspoon)
Black pepper, freshly ground (1/4 teaspoon)
Ground pork (1 pound)
Shiitake mushrooms, dried, chopped (2 cups)
Green onion stalks, chopped (12 pieces)
Cooking wine (2 tablespoons)
Salt (3/4 teaspoon)
Soy sauce (5 tablespoons)
Cornstarch (1 tablespoon)

Sauce:
Soy sauce (2 tablespoons)
Sesame seeds (1 tablespoon)
Balsamic vinegar (3 tablespoons)
Sesame oil (1 teaspoon)
Green pepper, diced (1/4 teaspoon)

Directions:

1. Plump up the dried mushrooms beforehand by soaking in a large bowl filled with water for four to eight hours. Once plumped up, place in the food processor. Add the yellow onions and green onions, and process until diced.

2. Fill a large bowl with the diced vegetables. Add the ground pork and mix with a fork. Stir in the sesame oil, cooking wine, salt, cornstarch, minced ginger, black pepper, soy sauce, and sugar. Place your well-combined meat mixture in the refrigerator to chill.

3. Meanwhile, place all the ingredients for the dipping sauce in a small bowl. Stir to combine; set aside.

4. Fill another large bowl with lukewarm water. Stir in the yeast; let stand for five minutes or until foamy. Stir in the rest of the ingredients for the buns. Knead to combine, cover with plastic wrap, and let sit on the counter for about four hours or until doubled in size.

5. Cover a cutting board with flour before rolling out ½ of the dough on it. Form into a log, cut into rounds, and roll to form 1-millimeter-thick disks. Fill the center of each bun with the meat mixture (1 ½ tablespoons) and fold at the top to form a filled bao bun.

6. Cover each bao bun at the bottom with a square of parchment paper. Cook in the steamer for about thirty to forty minutes or until cooked through. Serve right away with the dipping sauce.

7. Enjoy.

Barbecue Pork and Pickled Veggie Bao Buns

Ingredients:

Rice vinegar (1 tablespoon)
Milk (50 milliliters)
Caster sugar (1 ½ tablespoons + ¼ teaspoon)
Flour, plain (525 grams + ¼ cup for dusting)
Yeast, fast-action dried (1 teaspoon)
Coconut oil (1 tablespoon + 1 tablespoon for greasing + 2 tablespoons for brushing)
Baking powder (1 teaspoon)

Barbecue Pork:
Hoisin sauce (4 tablespoons)
Soy sauce, dark (2 tablespoons)
Tomato ketchup (4 tablespoons)

9. Place the carrot and mooli in a small bowl and stir together with the caster sugar and rice vinegar. Seal the jar before placing in the refrigerator for one hour.

10. Heat a large steamer on medium-high. Once the buns are done rising, place in the steamer and cook for eight minutes or until cooked through and puffed. Stuff each hot bao bun with divided portions of the barbecue pork and pickled vegetables. Top each with wasabi mayonnaise (a dollop) and spring onions (a pinch).

11. Serve and enjoy.

minutes. Roll out to form 3-millimeter-thick ovals before brushing oil on the surface. Place an oiled chopstick across each dough oval's center. After folding one edge of each dough over the opposite edge, carefully remove the chopstick. Place the bao buns on a parchment lined baking tray. Cover with cling film and leave in a warm spot for one hour and thirty minutes.

6. Meanwhile, fill a roasting tin with the pork. Combine the marinade ingredients and pour all over the pork. Rub the marinade onto the pork to coat it well, then cover with foil and refrigerate overnight.

7. The next day, set the oven at 320 degrees Fahrenheit to preheat. Remove the chilled pork from the refrigerator and cook in the oven for three hours and thirty minutes, making sure to baste the meat every hour.

8. Raise the oven temperature to 350 degrees Fahrenheit and then uncover the tin. Cook the pork for another forty-five minutes or until its edges are caramelized. Transfer the pork on a wire rack and allow to cool for twenty minutes. Slice into thin portions and place back in the tin. Mix the meat with the tin juices and keep warm.

Directions:

1. Place the flour inside a large bowl. Add the salt (1/2 teaspoon) and sugar and stir until well-combined.

2. Fill a small bowl with warm water (1 tablespoon), salt (a pinch), and yeast. Stir until evenly blended, and then pour into the flour mixture. Pour in the water (200 milliliters), oil, vinegar, and milk as well. Stir to combine everything into a soft sough.

3. Dust your work surface with a little flour. Transfer the dough onto it; knead for about ten to fifteen minutes or until elastic and smooth. Transfer the dough into a large oiled bowl. Cover with a towel and set on the kitchen counter; let the dough rise for two hours.

4. Once the dough has doubled in size, turn it out onto your flour-dusted work surface. Use your floured hands to flatten it into a disk. Dust the dough with the baking powder before kneading for five minutes and rolling into a 3-cemtimeter-thick log. Cut out 18 pieces of 3-centimeter-wide pieces from the dough log.

5. Mold each dough piece into rounds. Arrange on a large baking sheet and let sit for two to three

Coconut oil (2 tablespoons)
Garlic cloves, large, chopped finely (4 pieces)
Ginger, 2½-inch, peeled, chopped finely (1 piece)
Rice vinegar (2 tablespoons)
Caster sugar, golden (4 tablespoons)
Pork belly, rind-less (700 grams)

Garnish:
Pickled veggies – see below
Wasabi paste (1 teaspoon)
Spring onion, sliced diagonally into thin portions (5 pieces)
Mayonnaise (6 tablespoons)

Pickled Veggies:
Carrot, sliced into matchstick-sized portions (1 piece)
Caster sugar (3 tablespoons)
Mooli, peeled, sliced into matchstick-sized portions (1/2 piece)
Rice vinegar (3 tablespoons)

Bao Buns with Spicy Cider Pork Filling

Ingredients:

Pork:
Chicken stock, reduced sodium (500 milliliters)
Seasoning blend, Chinese 5-spice (2 teaspoons)
Scallions/spring onions, sliced diagonally into fine portions (4 pieces)
Pork belly, w/ skin removed (500 grams)
Cider (350 milliliters)
Hoisin sauce (100 grams)

Buns:
Yeast, dried (5 grams)
Flour, plain (75 grams)
Baking powder (1/2 teaspoon)
Salt (1/4 teaspoon)
Lard, chilled (25 grams)
Bread flour, white, strong (50 grams)
Caster sugar, golden (1 tablespoon)
Milk, whole (75 milliliters)
Coconut oil (1 tablespoon) – for greasing

Pickle:
Vinegar, regular/white wine (3 tablespoons)
Cucumber, sliced thinly (1 piece)
Sugar, light brown (1 teaspoon)

Directions:

1. Set the oven at 280 degrees Fahrenheit to preheat.

2. Meanwhile, rub a mixture of pepper and salt over the pork belly before sprinkling with the 5-spice.

3. Fill a medium-sized roasting tin (metal) with the seasoned pork belly and cover with the cider and chicken stock. Wrap the top of the tin with foil

before placing in the oven. Cook for about three hours or until the meat is tenderly coked and easily pulled apart with a fork. Allow the pork belly to sit in the stock as it cools.

4. Stir the salt, plain flour, and bread flour together in a large bowl. Cut the chilled lard into the flour mixture to give the latter a breadcrumbs-like consistency. Set aside.

5. Pour the milk into a saucepan heated on medium-low. Once the milk is warmed through, stir in the sugar and yeast. Let the yeast mixture sit for five minutes or until foamy. Add this milk mixture to the flour mixture and stir to combine. Use your hands to knead the entire mixture into a soft dough (or knead using the hook attachment of your stand mixer).

6. Transfer the dough into a large oiled bowl and cover with cling wrap. Then, let the dough rise for about one hour by just leaving on your kitchen counter (or somewhere else warm). Once the dough becomes twice its size, sprinkle all over with the baking powder. Knead with your hands to incorporate the baking powder into the dough before cutting into 8 equal sized bun shapes. Arrange on a large parchment-lined baking sheet,

cover with cling wrap, and leave on the counter for thirty minutes to allow for a second rising.

7. Sprinkle flour all over your work surface. Once the dough pieces are done with their second rise, transfer onto the work surface and roll each into 10-centimeter-long oval. Place each oval dough on a parchment paper square, brush on top with oil, fold across in half, and let sit for twenty minutes.

8. Meanwhile, line a baking tray with foil. Add the pork belly and set aside.

9. Pour the liquid from the roasting tin into a saucepan. Heat on medium to reduce the liquid to about 3/4 its original volume. Add the hoisin sauce and stir to combine with the sauce.

10. Set the grill on high. Meanwhile, brush the sauce onto the pork belly. Cook under the grill until a glaze form on the surface of the pork. Brush on the remaining sauce and cook under the grill for another four to five times or until you have a sticky, tasty pork belly.

11. Cook the buns for about six to eight minutes in the steamer. Work in batches to ensure the buns are cooked through and nicely puffed. Once done, transfer the buns onto a platter.

12. Combine the ingredients for the pickle and let sit for two minutes. Meanwhile, pull the pork belly into shreds with two forks.

13. Fill each steamed bao bun with the shredded pork. Finish by adding on the pickle. Serve garnished with red chili and enjoy right away.

Braised Pork Belly Bao Buns with Mustard Green and Chili Sauce

Ingredients:

Buns:
Flour, all purpose, unbleached (4 cups)
Sugar (2 tablespoons)
Salt (1/2 teaspoon)
Milk, warm (2 tablespoons + 1 ¼ cups)
Yeast, active dry (2 ¼ teaspoons)
Baking powder (2 ½ teaspoons)
Coconut oil (2 tablespoons)

Pork:
Garlic cloves, peeled, mashed lightly (5 pieces)
Sugar (2 tablespoons)
Cinnamon stick (1 piece)
Ginger, 2-inch, sliced (1 piece)
Kecap manis/caramel sauce, thick (2 tablespoons)
Pork belly, skin on, sliced into one-inch portions (2 ½ pounds)
Green onions, sliced into 3-inch long portions (5 pieces)
Oyster sauce (1 tablespoon)
Star anise (1 piece)
Soy sauce, light (3 tablespoons)
Water (3 cups + extra for blanching)

Mustard green:
Water, filtered
Salt
Rice vinegar
Mustard green, Chinese, including leaves & stems (6 pieces)

Chili sauce:
Garlic cloves (2 pieces)
Lime juice, freshly squeezed (1 teaspoon)
Sugar (1/4 cup)
Cornstarch (1/2 tablespoon) mixed with water (1/2 tablespoon)
Fresno chili, red, w/ seeds intact (1 piece)
Fresno chili, red, w/ seeds removed (1 piece)
Water (1/4 cup)
Rice vinegar (1 ½ tablespoons)
Salt (3/4 teaspoon)

Garnish:
Fresno chilies, red, sliced (2 pieces)
Peanuts/cashews, crushed (1/2 cup)
Cilantro sprigs (2 pieces)

Directions:

1. Place a layer of the mustard green at the bottom of a glass jar (wide-rimmed) and top with a thin layer of salt. Repeat with the remaining mustard green and salt, then cover with water, making sure the mustard green is submerged. Add the rice vinegar (1 tablespoon) before covering the jar and letting it ferment for about five to ten days. Just before serving, drain the mustard green and chop into bits.

2. Place the pork inside a large pot and over by 1" at the top with water. Heat on high to boiling, and then allow the meat to hard-boil for about one minute before draining and rinsing with cool water.

3. Fill another pot with garlic, ginger, green onions, soy sauce, oyster sauce, sugar, star anise, kecap manis/caramel sauce, cinnamon stick, and water (3 cups). Stir to combine before adding in the blanched pork. Heat to boiling, then reduce heat to a simmer, cover, and cook on low for another two hours. Uncover the pot and turn the heat up to medium-high. Allow the pork mixture to boil for twenty minutes or until the liquid is reduced to a thick sauce. Set aside.

4. Fill a small bowl with the yeast, warm milk, and sugar. Stir to combine and dissolve the yeast before letting stand for ten minutes. Meanwhile, pour the flour into a large bowl. Add the salt and baking powder; whisk well to combine. Pour in the yeast mixture and oil and mix into a soft dough. Transfer onto a flour-dusted surface and knead for about ten minutes or until elastic without being sticky.

5. Place the kneaded dough inside a large bowl greased with a little oil. Cover with cling wrap and leave on the counter to rise for one to two hours or until doubled in size. Knock out the dough with your fist before removing from the bowl. Turn it out on a flour-dusted surface and cut into 12 equal sized portions. Shape each dough piece into a 1/8-inch-thick disk.

6. Lightly brush the tops of the dough disks with oil before folding into half-moons and placing on parchment paper squares. Arrange on a baking sheet and cover with a clean kitchen towel. Leave for thirty minutes for a second rising.

7. Place the buns (with their parchment papers on) in the steamer, making sure to leave an inch of space between them, and cook for eight minutes or until puffed and cooked through. Remove from heat and let the steamed buns rest inside the

steamer for five minutes, before slowly opening the lid.

8. Fill the blender with the garlic cloves and chilies. Process into a well-combined paste and then transfer into a saucepan. Pour in the vinegar, water, lime juice, sugar, and salt. Stir to combine and heat to boiling. Reduce heat to low and stir in the cornstarch mixture. Continue cooking until the mixture thickens into chili sauce. Set aside.

9. Spread a little chili sauce on one side of each steamed bao bun. Add the pork on top, then drizzle with the prepared chili sauce. Finish by adding the mustard green, as well as the crushed nuts, sliced chilies, and cilantro.

10. Serve and enjoy.

Hoisin Ginger Pork Bao Buns with Dressed Slaw

Ingredients:

Pork:
Seasoning powder, 5-spice (2 tablespoons)
Garlic cloves, sliced (8 pieces)
Chili flakes, dried (1 teaspoon) OR chili flakes, smoked (1 teaspoon)
Ginger beer (1 cup)
Pork shoulder, w/ fat trimmed (3 kilograms)
Salt (1 tablespoon)
Pepper, freshly cracked (1 tablespoon)
Hoisin sauce (300 milliliters)

Buns:
Salt (1/4 teaspoon)
Yeast, instant dry (10 grams)
Milk powder (10 grams)
Baking soda (1/2 teaspoon)
Water, at room temp. (200 milliliters)
Cake flour (300 grams)
Caster sugar (4 tablespoons)
Baking powder (1/2 teaspoon)

Dressed slaw:
Sugar (1 teaspoon)
Rice vinegar (2 tablespoons)
Lemon juice, freshly squeezed (2 tablespoons)
Lime juice, freshly squeezed (2 tablespoons)
Cabbage, finely shredded (2 cups)

Directions:

1. Fill a small bowl with the five spice, salt, ginger, pepper, and chili. Mix well before rubbing all over the pork. Transfer the seasoned pork into your slow cooker pot; cover and let it marinate for one hour.

2. After one hour, add the ginger beer, hoisin sauce, and garlic to the slow cooker. Cover and cook on low for eight to nine hours or until the meat is extremely tender. Use two forks to shred the meat; mix with the juices and set aside.

3. Meanwhile, prepare the slaw by combining the lemon juice, lime juice, rice vinegar and sugar first, before tossing with the cabbage. Set aside.

4. Fill the bowl of your stand mixer with the yeast and water. Whisk until combined, then let sit for ten minutes or until the yeast is activated. Fit the paddle attachment to the mixer before pouring in the remaining dry ingredients to the bowl. Beat until well-blended, then replace the paddle with the dough hook attachment. Knead the mixture for five minutes and transfer onto a flour-dusted surface. Knead the dough into springy round shape.

5. Place the dough inside an oiled bowl and cover with plastic wrap. Let sit on the counter for one hour or until doubled in size. Punch down the dough before returning to the floured surface and rolling into a log. Slice into 12 disks and arrange on a flour-dusted baking tray. Cover with a kitchen towel and let the dough pieces rise for another thirty minutes or until done with their second rising.

6. Fold each dough disk across the center. Meanwhile, make 8x8-centimeter squares from a sheet of parchment paper. Top each square with one folded dough disk and place in the steamer. Working in batches, cover and cook for five minutes or until fully cooked and firm.

7. Place divided portions of the pickle and sliced cucumber on the bottom of each steamed bao bun. Top with the pulled pork and dressed cabbage slaw. Garnish with fresh coriander and serve immediately.

8. Enjoy.

Pickled Apple and Pork Belly Bao Buns

Ingredients:

Apple, red, cored, sliced thinly (1 piece)
Soy sauce (100 milliliters)
Kecap manis (6 tablespoons)
Yeast, fast action (5 grams)
Caster sugar, golden (30 grams + 75 grams)
Milk powder (2 tablespoons)
Cider vinegar (100 milliliters)
Star anise (1 piece)
Dry cider (6 tablespoons)
Honey (6 tablespoons)
White bread flour, strong (330 grams + ¼ cup for dusting)
Baking powder (1/4 teaspoon)
Olive oil, extra virgin (35 milliliters)
Pork belly, skinless, w/ fat trimmed (500 grams)
Dry cider (100 milliliters)
Coriander leaves (1 bunch) – for serving
Seasoning blend, Chinese five-spice (1/4 teaspoon + ¼ teaspoon)

Directions:

1. Set the oven at 320 degrees Fahrenheit to preheat.

2. Fill a small baking dish with the pork belly, as well as a mixture of water (200 milliliters), soy sauce, star anise, and cider. Add water as needed to cover the entire pork. Cover the dish with foil before placing in the oven. Cook for three hours.

3. Once the pork mixture is done, remove from the oven and let sit to cool in the juices. After one hour, discard the marinade and wrap the pork with cling wrap. Set aside to chill in the refrigerator.

4. Dissolve the yeast in warm water (180 milliliters); let stand for five minutes or until foamy. Meanwhile, fill the stand mixer bowl with the flour, baking powder, salt (1/2 teaspoon), milk powder, and sugar. Set the mixer at medium speed and combine the ingredients using the mixer's dough hook attachment. Add the yeast mixture and process for five minutes or until everything is combined into a round dough.

5. Gradually stream in the olive oil (35 milliliters) as you keep on kneading the dough for ten minutes. Once you have smooth and elastic dough, transfer

into a greased bowl. Cover with plastic wrap before letting sit on the counter for one hour or until it becomes twice the original size.

6. Once the dough is done rising, punch it down and then mold into 8 equal sized rounds. Arrange on a parchment paper lined baking tray and cover with plastic wrap. Let sit for a second rising on the counter for another half hour.

7. Meanwhile, fill a saucepan with the vinegar, five spice, sugar, and salt. Heat on medium and stir until well-blended. Let sit to cool before stirring in the apple. Pour into a medium bowl and allow to chill in the refrigerator.

8. Set the oven at 350 degrees Fahrenheit to preheat.

9. Fill a saucepan with the ingredients for the glaze. Stir to combine and heat on medium; allow the mixture to simmer for two minutes or until reduced into a syrup. Reserve 3 tablespoons of this syrup for serving later. Meanwhile, divide the remaining syrup into two portions; brush half on the pork and set the other half aside.

10. Place the glazed pork in the oven to cook for fifteen minutes. Brush the pork with the remaining

half of the glaze and return to the oven. Cook for another fifteen minutes or until caramelized on the surface. Let sit to cool before slicing into strips.

11. Once the dough pieces are done with the second rising, roll each into an oval and place in the steamer. Let sit for ten minutes before steaming for fifteen to twenty minutes or until cooked through and springy-soft.

12. Fill the steamed buns with divided portions of the pork strips, reserved sauce, and apple mixture. Serve sprinkled with coriander leaves.

Pork Bao Buns with Brussels Sprouts

Ingredients:

Pork belly, thick (1 slice)
Honey (2 tablespoons)
Brussels sprouts, w/ stems removed, halved (1/2 cup)
Peanuts, chopped (1/2 tablespoon)
Bao buns, steamed (3 pieces)
Coconut oil (4 cups) – for frying
Soy sauce (1 tablespoon)
Sriracha (1 tablespoon)

Directions:

1. Place the pork belly in the steamer and cook for five to ten minutes. Once completely cooked, place on a plate and let it dry out.

2. Heat a large skillet on medium. Pour in the oil and allow to heat through before adding the dry pork belly. Fry until cooked through and crispy,

transfer onto a plate lined with paper towels, sprinkle all over with salt, and allow to cool.

3. Fill a frying pan with oil. Add the Brussels sprouts, inner sides face down, and cook on high until browned. Stir in the soy sauce and reduce heat to medium. Cover and cook for two to three minutes or until the Brussels sprouts are softened.

4. Steam the bao buns until completely cooked. Place on a platter and keep warm by covering with a clean towel.

5. Mix the Sriracha and honey in a small bowl. Split each bao bun in the middle and fill with the Sriracha-honey mixture. Add the Brussels sprouts. Top with the crispy pork and chopped peanuts. Close each filled bao bun before serving right away.

Bao Buns Filled with Japanese Chashu Pork

Ingredients:

Ginger, 2-inch, peeled, sliced (1 piece)
Pork shoulder, ground (2 ½ pounds)
Sugar (1/4 cup)
Shallots, small, halved (2 pieces)
Mirin (1 cup)
Green onions (4 pieces)
Soy sauce (1/2 cup)
Sake (1 cup)
Garlic cloves, crushed (8 pieces)
Bao buns, steamed (5 pieces)

Directions:

1. Set the oven at 250 degrees Fahrenheit to preheat.

2. Fill a Dutch oven with all the ingredients (except the bao buns). Heat on medium to boiling, then cover and place inside the preheated oven. Allow the pork mixture to cook for about four to six hours, making sure to turn the pork halfway to ensure it cooks evenly and tenderly.

3. Meanwhile, arrange the steamed bao buns on a platter.

4. Transfer the pork onto a plate and slice into thin portions. Pour the juices all over the pork slices and stir to combine. Fill each bao bun with the tender-juicy sliced pork and serve immediately.

Chapter 2. Delectable Bao Buns with Beef Filling

Spicy Stir-Fried Beef Bao Buns

Ingredients:

Buns:
Milk, nonfat, dried (2 tablespoons)
Baking powder (1 ½ teaspoons)
Yeast, active dry (1/2 teaspoon)
Cake flour (3 ½ cups)
Coconut oil (1 tablespoon for greasing + 2 tablespoons for brushing)
Water, warmed to 115 degrees Fahrenheit, divided (1 cup)
Sugar (3 tablespoons + ¼ teaspoon)

Beef filling:
Corn flour (3 tablespoons)
Red chili, sliced thinly (1 piece)
Vinegar, rice wine/white wine (4 tablespoons)
Coconut oil (100 milliliters)
Tomato ketchup (2 tablespoons)
Garlic cloves, crushed (2 pieces)
Sweet chili sauce (2 tablespoons)
Minute steak, thin-cut, sliced into very thin strips (350 grams)
Seasoning powder, Chinese five-spice (2 teaspoons)

Red pepper, sliced thinly (1 piece)
Spring onions, divided into green & white parts, sliced (4 pieces)
Ginger, thumb-sized, julienned (1 piece)
Soy sauce (1 tablespoon)

Directions:

1. In a small bowl, combine the yeast, sugar (a pinch), and warm water (1/4 cup). Let sit for about five to ten minutes or until foamy. Add the dried milk and the remaining warm water (3/4 cup) and whisk well to combine. Set aside.

2. In a large bowl, stir together the flour and the remaining sugar (3 tablespoons). Once evenly blended, stir in the prepared yeast mixture. Use a fork to mix everything into a dough, then knead with clean hands.

3. Transfer the dough onto a surface that has been dusted with flour. Knead again for five minutes or until smooth and elastic, adding a little flour as needed to keep the dough from sticking. Mold the dough into a round shape before placing inside a large bowl greased with a little oil. After covering the bowl with plastic wrap, place on the counter and let sit for two hours or until the dough inside has doubled in size.

4. Knock down the dough before returning to your work surface, again dusted with a little flour. Shape the dough into a slightly flattened disk before sprinkling the baking powder over its center. With clean and flour-dusted hands, gather the dough by the edges and knead for five minutes or until it is evenly blended with the baking powder. Place the dough back in the oiled bowl, cover again with plastic wrap, and return to the counter for a second rising (about thirty minutes).

5. Meanwhile, cut out sixteen pieces of 3x2-inch wax paper rectangles. Brush lightly with oil and set aside.

6. Once the dough is done with its second rise, shape into a log that is about sixteen inches long. Cut into 16 portions before sprinkling all with flour, arranging on a large parchment-lined baking sheet, and covering with plastic wrap. After thirty minutes, roll each dough piece into a 6x3-inch oval. Fold each oval in half crosswise and set on a greased wax paper. Return the buns to the baking sheet, cover loosely with a towel, and let sit for another thirty minutes.

7. Working in batches, cook the buns in the steamer for about three minutes or until nicely puffed and fully cooked. Set the steamed buns on a plate after

removing their wax papers. Keep warm by covering with a kitchen towel.

8. Fill a large bowl with the beef. Add the five-spice and corn flour and toss to combine. Meanwhile, heat a large skillet on medium-high after filling it with the oil. Add the beef to the hot oil and cook until nicely crisp and golden. Transfer the beef onto a plate lined with paper towels.

9. Pour out the oil from the skillet, but leave one tablespoon of oil behind. Heat the skillet on medium, then stir in the garlic, spring onions (white ends), chili (1/2 portion), and ginger. Cook for about three minutes or until the garlic is softened.

10. Fill a small bowl with the soy sauce, ketchup, chilli sauce, water (2 tablespoons), and vinegar. Stir to combine, then pour this mixture all over the skillet vegetables. Allow the mixture to cook on simmer for two minutes before stirring in the beef. Gently toss until the beef is evenly coated.

11. Fill each warm bao bun with equal portions of the beef mixture. Serve and enjoy.

Beef Stew Bao Buns with Carrot Pickle

Ingredients:

Buns:
Peanut oil (1 tablespoon)
Sugar (30 grams)
Fennel seeds, toasted (1 tablespoon)
Yeast, dried (1 teaspoon)
Flour, plain (300 grams)
Salt (1/4 teaspoon)
Water, lukewarm (180 milliliters)

Beef stew:
Salt (1/4 teaspoon)
Garlic cloves, chopped finely (3 pieces)
White onion, sliced into half-inch cubes (1 piece)
Bouillon powder (1 teaspoon) dissolved in water (400 milliliters)
Brown sugar, soft (2 teaspoons)
Potato flour (2 tablespoons)
Red chili, w/ seeds removed, chopped finely (1 piece)
Carrots, small, sliced into half-inch circles (2 pieces)
Sriracha (1 teaspoon)
Stewing beef brisket, cut into half-inch chunks (400 grams)

White pepper, freshly ground (1/4 teaspoon)
Peanut oil (2 tablespoons)
Root ginger, fresh, 1-inch, chopped finely (1 piece)
Shallots, small, chopped finely (3 pieces)
Chinese 5-spice (1/2 teaspoon)
Tomatoes, medium, cored, quartered (4 pieces)
Chili bean paste (1 tablespoon)

Carrot pickle:
White turnip/daikon, 4-inch, finely grated (1 piece)
Mirin (2 tablespoons)
Caster sugar (1/4 teaspoon)
Carrot, medium, finely grated (1 piece)
Rice vinegar (2 tablespoons)
Sea salt, flaked (1/4 teaspoon)

Garnish:
Spring onions, sliced (1/4 cup)
Coriander leaves, fresh (1 bunch)

Directions:

1. Place all of the ingredients for the pickle in a medium bowl. Stir to combine, cover, and allow to chill in the refrigerator for twenty minutes or until ready to serve.

2. Fill a large bowl with the flour, yeast, water, salt, and sugar. Stir to combine before kneading for ten to twelve minutes or until combined into an elastic dough. Transfer into an oiled bowl and cover with plastic wrap, then leave on the counter for three hours to let it rise. Once the dough has doubled in size, knock down and sprinkle on top with the fennel seeds. Knead gently to incorporate the seeds into the dough.

3. Portion the dough into 16 rounds. Place on a flour-dusted baking sheet, cover with plastic wrap, and leave on the counter to rest for twenty minutes.

4. In the meantime, mix the white pepper and salt with the beef. Sprinkle all over with potato flour.

5. Fill a skillet with a little oil and heat on high. Add the seasoned beef and cook until browned and caramelized all over. Drag the beef to one side of the skillet, then fill the space with more oil. Once hot, add the onions, garlic, shallots, ginger, and

chillies. Stir and cook until lightly browned, before stirring in the rest of the beef stew ingredients. Cover and allow the beef mixture to cook on medium for one hour and thirty minutes.

6. Turn the heat down to low and, stirring occasionally, let the beef stew cook for an additional twenty minutes or until nicely thickened.

7. Meanwhile, add the buns to your steamer, making sure to leave a quarter of an inch of space between them. Cover the steamer and let the buns cook until puffed and evenly done. Transfer the steamed buns onto a platter.

8. Pour the beef stew into a serving bowl and top with spring onions and coriander. Serve with the bao bun platter and enjoy right away.

Braised Short Rib Bao Buns with Pickled Vegetables

Ingredients:

Old dough:
Yeast, dried, fast-action (4 grams)
Flour, plain (300 grams + ¼ cup for dusting)
Milk/water, lukewarm (140 milliliters)

New dough:
Yeast, dried, fast-action (10 grams)
Caster sugar (60 grams)
Coconut oil (20 milliliters + 2 tablespoons for brushing + 1 tablespoon for greasing)
Flour, plain (500 grams)
Salt (1/2 teaspoon)
Baking powder (1/2 teaspoon)
Water/milk, lukewarm (290 milliliters)

Filling:
Beef short ribs, separated (1 ½ kilograms)
Vinegar, Chinese rice wine (1 ½ tablespoons)
Onion, large, sliced into quarters (1 piece)
Caster sugar (1/2 teaspoon)
Coconut oil – for frying
Garlic cloves (6 pieces)
Soy sauce (5 tablespoons)

Shaoxing wine (240 milliliters)

Pickled vegetables:

Carrots, medium, peeled (2 pieces)

Caster sugar (50 grams)

Daikon, small, peeled (1 piece)

Vinegar, Chinese rice wine (100 milliliters)

Salt (1 teaspoon)

For serving:

Mayonnaise

Coriander leaves, chopped

Directions:

1. Pour the ingredients for the old dough into a large bowl. Stir to combine with salt (just a pinch) and then create a well in the mixture's center. Fill the well with water/milk, and then combine everything into a soft dough. Transfer the dough into a surface that has been dusted with flour. Knead the dough for three to four minutes or until elastic. Place dough inside a greased bowl and cover with cling wrap. Set aside on the counter to let the dough rise for three hours or so.

2. Prepare the new dough as you had done with the old dough. Your new dough will turn out having a drier consistency than the old dough. Place the new dough on your flour-dusted work surface and

knead until smooth. Once the old dough has doubled in size, place it on top of the new dough. Knead them together for about three to four minutes or until well-blended and soft. Place the dough in the greased bowl, cover with wrap, and set on the counter for a second rising.

3. Set the oven at 320 degrees Fahrenheit to preheat. Meanwhile, combine the shaoxing with vinegar and soy sauce; set aside.

4. Heat a large skillet on high before pouring in the coconut oil. Once heated through, add the short ribs and cook for one to two minutes or until browned all over. Transfer the ribs into a roasting tin, making sure the ribs fit snugly inside. Meanwhile, add the onion and garlic to the skillet. Stir and cook for about two to three minutes or until softened and fragrant, then pour on top of the ribs. Pour on the shaoxing mixture as well as enough water to cover the ribs a quarter of the way. Secure the dish with foil before roasting in the oven for about three hours and thirty minutes or until tenderly cooked.

5. Fill a medium bowl with the cold water (50 milliliters), sugar, vinegar, and salt; stir to combine. Meanwhile, grate the carrots and daikon in the food processor before adding to the pickling

juice. Cover and let sit at room temperature for one hour. Discard the liquid and then allow to chill in the refrigerator until ready to serve.

6. Transfer the roasted ribs onto a platter. Allow to slightly cool before carving the meat and discarding the bones. Meanwhile, pour the cooking liquid from the roasting tin into a saucepan; heat on high and let the juice cook for ten minutes or until thick and syrupy. Pour the sauce all over the carved meat, toss to coat and combine, cover with foil, and set aside.

7. Transfer the dough onto a floured surface. Roll into a log shape before cutting and molding into 32 balls. Gently flatten each dough ball to form a disk, then lightly brush with oil and fold across in half. Place all dough buns on a large baking sheet and cover with a towel. Allow the buns to rise for fifteen minutes before steaming for fifteen minutes or until cooked through and puffed.

8. After opening each steamed bao bun, spread its bottom half with the mayonnaise. Top with the saucy meat, pickle, and chopped coriander. Serve and enjoy right away.

Beefy Hawaiian Style Bao Buns

Ingredients:

Buns:
Flour, all purpose (3 cups + ¼ for dusting)
Honey (3 tablespoons)
Sesame oil, toasted (2 teaspoons + 1 tablespoon for greasing)
Water, warmed to 105-115 degrees Fahrenheit (3/4 cup)
Active dry yeast (1/4 ounce)
Kosher salt (1/2 teaspoon)

Filling:
Ground beef, 80/20 (8 ounces)
Hoisin sauce (2 tablespoons)
Five-spice blend, Chinese (3/4 teaspoon)
Yellow onion, small, diced (1 piece)
Soy sauce (2 tablespoons)
Coconut oil (2 teaspoons + 1 tablespoon for greasing)
Kosher salt (1/4 teaspoon)
Black pepper, freshly ground (1/4 teaspoon)
Garlic cloves, minced (2 pieces)
Dry sherry (3 tablespoons)

Directions:

1. Fill a small bowl with the honey and warm water. Whisk well to combine before sprinkling in the yeast. Keep stirring until the yeast is completely dissolved, and then let sit for four to six minutes or until foaming.

2. Fill a large bowl with the flour. Stir in the salt before pouring in the sesame oil and prepared yeast mixture. Using a wooden spoon, stir everything together until well-blended into a doughy texture. Sprinkle on a little flour, if needed, to keep the dough from being sticky, before kneading for five minutes or until elastic and smooth.

3. Use sesame oil (1 tablespoon) to grease a large bowl. Meanwhile, gather the dough into a ball and then place inside the oiled bowl. Use a clean towel to cover the dough as it rests somewhere warm for about one hour or until double in size.

4. Stir a mixture of the black pepper and salt into the ground beef. Meanwhile, heat a medium-sized skillet (nonstick) on medium-high. Pour in the coconut oil; once heated through, add the seasoned ground meat and cook for about two minutes or until the meat is broken up to bits, lightly browned, and just about cooked. Set aside on a plate.

5. Turn the heat down to medium as you fill the same skillet with the onion. Stir and cook for eight minutes or until lightly browned. Stir in the garlic and cook for two minutes or until softened, before adding the beef back to the skillet. Add the five spice, then give the mixture a good stir for half a minute, before stirring in the sherry. Allow the mixture to cook until almost dry. Stir in the water (1/4 cup), hoisin sauce, and soy sauce. Continue cooking for three minutes or until you have a nicely thickened sauce. Remove from heat and set aside to completely cool.

6. Meanwhile, sprinkle a little flour all over our work surface, cut out 8 3-inch squares from a sheet of wax paper, and brush a little oil onto a baking sheet.

7. Once the dough is done rising, transfer onto your flour-dusted surface and punch down with your fist. Slice the dough into 8 rounds before rolling into 5-inch-diameter disks. After cupping each piece of dough in your hand, fill its center with two tablespoons of the prepared filling. Seal each filled bun by pinching around the edges, flip it over onto a greased wax paper square, and smoothen with your hands into a dome.

8. Place all of the filled bao buns on the greased baking sheet, making sure they are evenly spaced apart. Cover with a clean kitchen towel and leave somewhere warm for a second rising.

9. Meanwhile, pour enough water into a large pot to fill it about three inches from the bottom. Heat on medium-high and bring to a gentle boil.

10. After forty-five minutes to one hour, or once the buns are plumped to twice their size, add the buns to your steamer insert (do this in batches), making sure there is a one-inch gap between each bun (to allow for room to expand as they cook). Cover and cook for about twenty minutes or until springy and cooked through, then serve immediately.

Bulgogi Beef Bao Buns

Ingredients:

Carrots, shredded (1/4 cup)
Beef, sliced thinly (1/2 pound)
Radish/burdock root, sliced, pickled (6 pieces)
Bao buns, steamed (3 pieces)
Bulgogi marinade (1/2 cup)
Quick pickles (6 pieces)
Cilantro sprigs (2 pieces)

Directions:

1. Fill a large bowl with the bulgogi marinade. Add the beef slices and let sit to marinate for two to three hours.

2. Meanwhile, set the grill on medium-high to preheat.

3. Remove the beef slices from the marinade and place on the hot grill. Cook for five minutes on each side or until nicely marked and cooked through.

4. Once the buns are steamed and nicely puffed, open each carefully and fill with divided portions of the cooked beef slices. Slather on the kewpie mayonnaise before topping with the pickled burdock root, pickled cucumbers, and shredded carrots.

5. Serve garnished with cilantro sprigs and enjoy.

Chapter 3. Scrumptious Bao Buns with Chicken/Turkey Filling

Fried Chicken and Milk Gravy Bao Buns

Ingredients:

Buns:
Sea salt (1 teaspoon)
Sugar (2 teaspoons)
Milk (1 ¼ cups)
Bread flour (4 ¾ cups)
Honey (6 tablespoons)
Yeast, dry active (2 teaspoons)

Chicken:
Buttermilk (3 cups)
Paprika (1 teaspoon)
Pepper, freshly cracked (1 teaspoon)
Sea salt (1 teaspoon)
Chicken breasts (2 pounds)
Cayenne (1 teaspoon)
Flour (1 ½ cups)
Garlic powder (1 teaspoon)
Coconut oil – for frying

Gravy:
Milk (1 ¾ cups)
Flour (1/4 cup)
Butter (1 tablespoon)
Duck fat (1/4 cup)
Salt (1/4 teaspoon)
Pepper, freshly cracked (1/4 teaspoon)

Garnish:
Cilantro (1 bunch)
Avocados, ripe, mashed (2 pieces)

Directions:

1. After slicing the chicken into 1x3-inch tenders, place inside a large bowl filled with cayenne (1 teaspoon) and buttermilk (3 cups). Stir to combine, making sure the chicken tenders are evenly coated. Cover the bowl with plastic wrap before refrigerating overnight.

2. Meanwhile, fill a small saucepan with the milk. Heat on low; once the milk is warm, remove from heat. Whisk in the yeast and sugar (2 teaspoons) and then let sit for eight minutes or until the yeast is activated.

3. Fill the bowl of your stand mixer with the flour, honey, salt, and yeast mixture. Process for ten minutes on medium speed or until well-combined into a doughy consistency. Transfer the dough into a large bowl greased with oil and cover with cling wrap. Let sit in a warm area for one hour and thirty minutes or until doubled in size.

4. Once the dough has risen to twice its size, knock down with your fist and transfer onto a surface dusted with flour. Roll the dough and shape into a log before cutting into 12 portions. Mold each dough piece into a ball and then press into a 3x7-inch oval. Cover half of each oval dough piece with parchment before folding the other half of the dough over it, then covering the bottom of the dough with another piece of parchment. Arrange your dough half-moons on a large baking sheet that has been lined with baking paper. Cover with cling wrap and let sit on the counter for forty-five minutes.

5. Fit a bamboo steamer inside a wok. Pour in water and heat on medium; once simmering, add the buns in batches and steam for ten minutes or until cooked and puffed. Set the steamed buns on a wire rack and allow to cool.

6. Place the duck fat in a saucepan heated on medium. Once melted, whisk in the flour; keep whisking for one minute and then add the milk. Whisk to combine and allow the mixture to cook on simmer until thickened. Whisk in the pepper, salt, and butter to finish the milk gravy. Set aside.

7. Heat a Dutch oven to 350 degrees Fahrenheit after filling it with oil. Meanwhile, fill a large bowl with flour, pepper, garlic, salt, and paprika. Stir to combine before dredging in the chicken tenders. Drop the coated chicken pieces in batches into the hot oil and fry for about six to eight minutes or until cooked through and nicely golden. Once done, place chicken tenders on a plate lined with paper towels and allow to drain out excess oil as they cool.

8. Slather avocado (1 tablespoon) onto each steamed bun's base before topping with chicken tenders (2 pieces) and milk gravy (a dollop). Serve your bao buns garnished with cilantro sprigs.

Gojuchang Chicken Bao Buns with Bahn Mi Slaw

Ingredients:

Gojuchang chicken:
Sesame seeds (1/2 tablespoon)
Honey (3 tablespoons)
Mirin (1 tablespoon)
儀 ilantro, chopped (1/4 cup)
Soy sauce (2 tablespoons)
Lime juice, freshly squeezed (2 tablespoons)
Gojuchang (1/4 cup)
Brown sugar (2 tablespoons)
Rice wine vinegar (2 tablespoons)
Hoisin sauce (1/2 cup)
Chicken tenders (1 pound)

Bahn mi slaw:
Salt, kosher (1/4 teaspoon)
Pepper, freshly cracked (1/4 teaspoon)
Jalapeno, w/ seeds removed, sliced (1 piece)
Rice wine vinegar (1/4 cup)
Red bell pepper, sliced (1/2 piece)
Cilantro leaves, fresh (1 cup)
Sesame oil (1/4 cup)
Green cabbage, shredded (2 cups)
Carrot matchsticks (1 cup)
Cucumber, sliced (1/2 cup)
Radish, sliced (2 pieces)
Sesame seeds (2 tablespoons)
Honey (1 tablespoon)

Bao buns:
Bread flour, sifted (3 cups + ¼ cup for kneading)
Rice wine vinegar (2 tablespoons)
Caster sugar (5 tablespoons)
Baking powder (2 teaspoons)
Water, warmed to 112 to 115 degrees Fahrenheit (2 cups)
Active yeast (1 tablespoon)
Cornstarch, sifted (1 cup)
Coconut oil (2 tablespoons)

Directions:

1. Place the honey, soy sauce, lime juice, hoisin sauce, rice wine vinegar, mirin, gojuchang, cilantro, sesame seeds, and brown sugar inside a large bowl. Whisk well to combine before adding in the chicken. Coat the chicken well with the marinade and then place in the refrigerator to chill overnight.

2. Heat a griddle pan on medium-high. Take the chicken pieces out of their marinade and add to the hot pan. Cook on each side for about three to four minutes or until completely cooked and nicely marked. Allow the chicken to rest for two to three minutes, then slice into thin portions.

3. In a medium bowl, stir all the ingredients for the bahn mi slaw together until well-combined. Place in the refrigerator to chill before serving.

4. Fill a large bowl, with yeast, sugar, and water. Whisk to combine and set aside for five to seven minutes or until the yeast mixture becomes foamy. Add the bread flour, baking powder, cornstarch, shortening, and rice wine vinegar and stir to combine until the ingredients come together into a dough. Transfer the dough onto a flour-dusted surface and knead for about ten minutes or until soft and elastic. Place inside a greased bowl, cover

with cling film, and let sit on the counter for one hour or until doubled in size.

5. Once the dough is done rising, return to the floured surface and dust on top with the baking powder. Knead gently for two to three minutes before placing back in the greased bowl. Cover with cling wrap and set aside on the counter for a second rising. After thirty minutes, return the dough to your floured work surface and mold into 20 rounds. Transfer onto a parchment-lined baking tray and cover with cling wrap. Allow the dough balls to rest for fifteen minutes.

6. Shape each dough ball into a 5-inch-long oval before brushing on top with oil. Fold all dough pieces to form taco-like shells and place in the steamer. Cook for about four to six minutes or until cooked through and fluffy.

7. Fill each steamed bao bun shell with the chicken and bahn mi slaw. Serve immediately.

Chicken and Mushroom Bao Buns

Ingredients:

Buns:
Coconut oil (1/2 tablespoon)
Milk (1/2 cup)
Steamed bun flour (8 ounces)
Sugar (1/4 cup)
Lime juice, freshly squeezed (1/4 teaspoon)

Filling:
Fish sauce (1/2 teaspoon)
Napa cabbage leaf, shredded finely (1 piece)
Sugar (1/2 teaspoon)
Cilantro leaves, coarsely chopped (a handful)
Bouillon powder, chicken (1/4 teaspoon)
Chicken breast, boneless, skinless, sliced into half-inch chunks (8 ounces)
Shiitake mushrooms, dried (2 pieces)
Cornstarch (3/4 teaspoon)
Salt (1/4 teaspoon)
White pepper powder (3 dashes)

Directions:

1. Pour the steamed bun flour into a large bowl. Add the oil, milk, and sugar. Stir to combine for

about five minutes or until the mixture becomes a smooth and soft dough. Use floured hands to roll the dough until it is shaped into a 1½-inch-in-diameter cylinder. Place on a floured baking sheet, cover with a dampened towel, and let sit.

2. Fill a medium bowl with hot water. Add the dried shiitake mushrooms and set aside to soak until softened. Slice thinly in to strips.

3. Meanwhile, fill a large bowl with the ingredients for the bao bun filling. Stir to combine and set aside.

4. Cut out 1½x1½-inch parchment squares. Set aside.

5. Cut the log of dough onto one-inch-thick pieces before flattening with a rolling pin. Fill the center of each piece of dough with the prepared chicken filling (1 teaspoon) before pleating the dough and pinching around the edges to seal. Set each filled bun on a parchment square before placing inside the steamer.

6. After ensuring that the buns are evenly spaced apart inside the steamer, steam for ten minutes or until evenly cooked and springy to the touch. Immediately transfer onto a platter and serve.

Easy Bao Buns with Spicy Chicken Filling

Ingredients:

Bao buns:
Cornstarch (1/4 cup)
Water, warmed to 120 degrees Fahrenheit (1 cup)
Sugar (2 tablespoons)
Black sesame seeds (1 teaspoon)
Green onions, sliced (1 tablespoon)
Flour, all purpose (2 ¾ cups)
Yeast, active dry (1 packet)
Salt (3/4 teaspoon)

Spicy Chicken:
Chicken thighs, skinless, boneless, chopped finely (12 ounces)
Tamari/soy sauce (2 tablespoons)
Brown sugar (1 tablespoon)
Coconut oil (2 teaspoons)
Hoisin sauce (1 tablespoon)
Chinese 5-spice (1 teaspoon)
Rice wine vinegar (3 tablespoons)
Chili garlic sauce (2 tablespoons)
Oyster sauce (1 tablespoon)
Cornstarch (2 teaspoons)

Directions:

1. In a large bowl, combine the cornstarch, rice wine vinegar, brown sugar, chile garlic, five spice, hoisin sauce, and soy sauce. Toss in the chicken, making sure it is well-coated. Cover and refrigerate.

2. Fill a separate large bowl with the flour (2 cups), sugar, cornstarch, salt, and un-dissolved yeast. Pour in the warm water and stir to combine everything into a soft dough. Transfer the dough onto a surface that has been dusted with flour. With floured hands, knead the dough for about four to six minutes or until elastic and smooth. Place in an oiled bowl, cover with a kitchen towel, and allow the dough to rest for ten minutes.

3. Heat a large nonstick skillet on medium-high after filling with oil. Drain out the marinade before placing the chicken in the hot oil. Cook for about five to seven minutes or until completely cooked. Transfer onto a paper towel-lined plate and allow to cool.

4. Meanwhile, line the steamer basket with parchment, then lightly brush with oil.

5. After punching the dough, cut into 16 four-inch rounds. Top the center of each dough piece with

chicken (1 tablespoon) and cover with the edges of the dough, pinching the seams on top to seal. Set each filled bun on a piece of parchment and place in the steamer basket.

6. Cook the filled buns for about twelve to fifteen minutes or until fully cooked. Serve topped with green onions and sesame seeds, alongside the reserved dipping sauce.

7. Enjoy.

Black Pepper Turkey Bao Buns

Ingredients:

Buns:
Corn muffin mix (1 cup)
Yeast, active dry (2 ¼ teaspoons)
Baking powder (1 teaspoon)
Sugar (2 tablespoons)
Flour, all purpose (2 cups)
Salt, kosher (1 tablespoon)
Coconut oil (2 tablespoons + 1 tablespoon)

Black Pepper Sauce:
Black pepper, freshly ground (1 teaspoon)
Soy sauce, regular (3 tablespoons + 2 tablespoons)
Ginger, 1½-inch, peeled, sliced thinly (1 piece)
Rice vinegar, unseasoned (2 teaspoons)
Sugar (1/4 cup)
Thai chile, green/red, sliced thinly (1 piece)
Garlic clove, sliced thinly (1 piece)
Mushroom soy sauce (2 tablespoons)

For serving:
Mayonnaise
Carrots, shredded
Pickles
Cilantro leaves, including stems
Turkey breast, grilled, pastrami style

Directions:

1. In a small bowl, stir the yeast and sugar together with warm water (2/3 cup). Allow the yeast to activate within five minutes.

2. In a large bowl, whisk the flour together with the baking powder, salt, and corn muffin mix. Add the yeast mixture and stir to combine. Add the oil (2 tablespoons) and knead until you have a doughy mixture.

3. Sprinkle flour all over your work surface before turning out the dough mixture onto it. Knead until smooth, and then transfer into a bowl coated with a little oil inside. Cover with a kitchen towel and set somewhere warm. Let the dough rise for one hour and thirty minutes or until elastic and puffy.

4. Fill a saucepan with the soy sauce (3 tablespoons) and sugar. On medium heat, stir and cook for five minutes or until the sugar is completely dissolved. Pour the mixture into a small bowl. Stir in the remaining sauce (2 tablespoons), mushroom soy sauce, chile, garlic, pepper, ginger, and vinegar. Set aside for thirty minutes.

5. Once the dough is done rising, shape into sixteen 6x3-inch smooth oval pieces. Fold each in half to form crescents and place in a parchment-lined baking sheet. Cover with a kitchen towel and return to the warm spot for a second rising. Within one hour and thirty minutes.

6. Add the bao buns to your steamer basket. Cook by batches for ten to twelve minutes or until completely cooked and firm. Transfer onto a platter and fill each bun with equal portions of the turkey. Top with mayonnaise, carrots, and pickles before drizzling with the black pepper sauce.

7. Serve garnished with cilantro and enjoy.

Bao Buns with Chicken and Chives Stuffing

Ingredients:

Buns:
Sugar (1/8 cup)
Lard, melted (1/2 tablespoon)
Water, lukewarm (5 tablespoons)
Water, warm (3/4 cup)
Yeast, dry (1/2 tablespoon)
Flour, all purpose, sifted (2 ½ cups)

Stuffing:
Garlic, minced (1 tablespoon)
Chicken meat, ground (2 cups)
Shiitake mushrooms, sliced (2 cups)
Truffle oil (1 tablespoon)
Coconut oil – for cooking
Ginger, minced (1 tablespoon)
Salt (1/4 teaspoon)
Black pepper, freshly ground (1/4 teaspoon)
Chives, chopped (1/3 cup)

Directions:

1. Fill a small bowl with warm water and sugar. Stir to completely dissolve the sugar before stirring in the yeast as well. Let the mixture sit for ten minutes or until foamy. Stir in the lard before pouring into the food processor.

2. Add flour to the food processor. Keep it running as you gradually stream in the water. Once the mixture comes together into a soft ball, transfer onto a floured surface. Knead the dough for ten minutes before rolling out to form a 2-inch-thick log. Slice the log of dough into 2-inch disks. Set aside to let the buns rest.

3. Add oil to a sauté pan after heating it on medium. Stir in the garlic and ginger. Add the shiitake mushrooms, pepper, and salt and stir to combine. Cook until the mushrooms are softened, and then set aside to cool. Once the mushroom mixture has cooled, transfer into a large bowl filled with the chives and truffle oil. Add the chicken, salt, and pepper and stir until well-blended. Allow to chill in the refrigerator for thirty minutes.

4. Scoop out one tablespoon of the chicken and chives filling and stuff into a bun. Gather the edges of the bun toward the top and lightly pinch. Repeat

with the remaining buns and filling. Arrange the filled buns in a parchment-lined sheet and let sit for thirty minutes.

5. Add the filled buns to the steamer basket. Cover and cook for about ten to twelve minutes or until puffed and cooked through.

6. Serve and enjoy.

Turkey and Kimchi Filled Bao Buns

Ingredients:

Ginger, 1-inch, peeled, minced (1 piece)
Bao buns, frozen, steamed (6 pieces)
English cucumber, sliced thinly into rounds (1 piece)
Chili flakes, Korean (1 ¼ tablespoons)
Garlic cloves, peeled, minced (3 pieces)
Sugar (2 tablespoons)
Ground turkey (10 ounces)
Radish, trimmed, sliced into rounds (6 ounces)
Scallions, trimmed, sliced thinly at an angle, w/ green & white parts separated (3 pieces)
Rice wine vinegar (2 tablespoons)
Ground bean sauce (2 tablespoons)

Directions:

1. Fill a large bowl with the cucumber, radish, garlic (1/2 portion), sugar (1/2 portion), ginger (1/2 portion), scallion green parts (1/2 portion), gochugaru (1/2 portion), olive oil (a drizzle), and vinegar. Stir to combine before seasoning with pepper and salt. Let the kimchi marinate for ten minutes.

2. Meanwhile, add oil (2 teaspoons) to a nonstick skillet heated on medium-high. Stir in the ground turkey, pepper, and salt. Cook for about six to eight minutes or until cooked through and browned. Pour into a bowl and set aside, but leave the browned bits in the pan.

3. Add more oil (2 teaspoons) to the same pan. Heat on medium, then stir in the scallion white parts as well as the remaining half portions of the garlic and ginger. Cook for one minute or until fragrant and softened before stirring in the cooked turkey, water (1/2 cup), ground bean sauce, and remaining half portions of sugar and gochugaru. Cook for four to six minutes or until nicely thickened. Stir in pepper and salt to taste and set aside.

4. Set a strainer/colander on top of a pot filled with boiling water. Fill the strainer/colander with the frozen bao buns and steam for three to five minutes or until nicely puffed and softened. Place steamed buns on a platter.

5. Stuff each steamed bao bun with the kimchi and turkey mixture. Serve topped with the remaining scallion green parts and enjoy.

Bao Buns with Curry Fried Chicken Filling

Ingredients:

Red onion, pickled (1 tablespoon)
Mint leaves, fresh (3 pieces)
Bao buns, frozen, steamed (3 pieces)
Mayonnaise, kewpie (1 tablespoon)
Cabbage, lime-y (3 tablespoons)

Cabbage:
Sugar (1 teaspoon)
Curry fried chicken (1 breast) – see below
Red cabbage, shaved (3 tablespoons)
Lime juice, freshly squeezed (2 tablespoons)

Chicken:
Milk (1 splash)
Panko breadcrumbs (1 cup)
Ginger (1 teaspoon)
Curry (1 ½ tablespoons)
Egg (1 piece)
Chicken breast (1 piece)
Cornstarch (1 teaspoon)
Salt (1 teaspoon)
Turmeric (1 teaspoon)
Coconut oil – for frying

Directions:

1. Place the cabbage in a medium bowl filled with sugar and lime juice. Toss to combine.

2. Meanwhile, fill a small bowl with the curry (1 tablespoon), turmeric, ginger, and salt. Stir to combine before slathering all over the chicken breast. Set aside for about thirty minutes.

3. Place the remaining curry in another small bowl; add the panko, salt, and cornstarch and toss until well-mixed. Meanwhile, whisk the egg together with the milk.

4. After steaming the buns, keep warm on a plate covered with a warm, dampened towel. Meanwhile, pour the oil into a large skillet and heat to 370 degrees Fahrenheit.

5. Dip the marinated chicken into the seasoned panko before coating with the egg wash. Dip again in the panko and then gently drop into the hot oil. Fry until crispy and cooked through, then place on a paper towel lined plate.

6. Open each warm bun and cover the base with kewpie mayonnaise. Add the cabbage, chicken, and pickled red onions. Serve garnished with mint leaves and enjoy.

Spicy Chicken Katsu Bao Buns

Ingredients:

Sambal (1 tablespoon)
Butter (1 pat)
Cilantro sprigs (2 pieces)
Bao buns, frozen, steamed (3 pieces)
Sesame seeds, toasted (1 tablespoon)
Quick pickles (6 pieces)
Chicken katsu (1 piece) – see below

Chicken:
Cornstarch (2 tablespoons)
Flour (1/2 cup)
Egg, whisked (1 piece)
Chicken breast (1 piece)
Salt (1/4 teaspoon)
Pepper, freshly cracked (1/4 teaspoon)
Panko breadcrumbs, seasoned (1/2 cup)

Directions:

1. Slice the chicken into 3 portions before adding to a large bowl filled with salt, pepper, and cornstarch. Toss to combine, making sure the chicken pieces are evenly coated.

2. Pour the oil into a large nonstick skillet. Heat to 370 degrees Fahrenheit.

3. Dredge the chicken pieces in flour, egg wash, and panko before adding to the hot oil. Cook until fully cooked and nicely crisp. Set aside on a plate.

4. Meanwhile, cook the frozen buns in the steamer. Set aside on a plate covered with a steamed towel.

5. Heat a small skillet on medium after filling with butter. Once the butter melts, top with the steamed buns. After one minute, remove from the skillet and set on a platter. Sprinkle sesame seeds on top.

6. Stuff the buns with divided portions of the chicken. Top with sambal, cucumbers, and cilantro before serving.

7. Enjoy right away.

Teriyaki Turkey Bao Buns

Ingredients:

Braised turkey slices, cooked (3 pieces)
Pineapple slices (3 pieces)
Mayonnaise, kewpie (1 tablespoon)
Bao buns, frozen/homemade, steamed (3 pieces)
Teriyaki sauce (1 tablespoon)
Nori slices (3 pieces)

Directions:

1. Steam the buns until puffed, then keep warm by placing on a plate covered with a steamed towel.

2. Mist a frying pan with cooking spray and heat on medium. Add the turkey slices and let them brown and crisp up. Brush on all sides with the teriyaki and cook for another thirty seconds. Set aside on a plate.

3. Spread the kewpie mayonnaise on the inside of each steamed bun before filling with the turkey and pineapple. Wet the nori and press one slice onto the top of each bun.

4. Serve and enjoy with your favorite dipping sauce.

Peking Chicken Bao Buns

Ingredients:

Salt, kosher (2 teaspoons) OR table salt (1 teaspoon)
Five-spice powder (1 ½ teaspoons)
Rice wine/dry sherry (1 teaspoon)
Soy sauce, dark (3 tablespoons)
Rice vinegar (1 teaspoon)
Chicken breasts, w/ skin on (4 pieces)
Ginger slices, mashed (3 pieces)
Sesame oil (1 teaspoon)
Brown sugar (2 tablespoons)
Black pepper, freshly ground (1/2 teaspoon)
Steamed buns (4 pieces)

Directions:

1. Place the marinade ingredients in a small bowl and whisk to combine. Meanwhile, prick the chicken skin and meat with a fork to create holes for the marinade to penetrate. Cover the chicken with the marinade and let sit for four hours.

2. Set the oven at 400 degrees Fahrenheit to preheat. Meanwhile, place the steamed buns on a platter covered with a warm and moist towel.

3. Remove the chicken from its marinade and pat dry with paper towels. Add the chicken, skin side down, to a Dutch oven filled with oil (3 tablespoons) and heated on high. Cook for three minutes or until crisp and golden, and then flip the chicken onto the other side. Quickly place the Dutch oven into the preheated oven; allow the chicken to continue cooking for about fifteen minutes or until tenderly cooked through.

4. Transfer the chicken onto a cutting board. Let sit for ten minutes before slicing into half-inch thick strips.

5. Pour the remaining marinade into a small saucepan and heat on medium-high. Allow it to reduce and thicken into a sauce.

6. Place one piece of chicken inside each steamed bun. Drizzle with the sauce and serve immediately.

Chapter 4. Tasty Bao Buns with Fish/Seafood Filling

Spicy Popcorn Shrimp Bao Buns

Ingredients:

Bao buns, frozen (12 pieces)
Green onions, chopped (a handful)
Popcorn shrimp, frozen (1 package)
Carrot, shredded (1 cup)
Mayonnaise, kewpie (1/4 cup)

Sauce:
Ginger, minced (1 teaspoon)
Soy sauce (4 tablespoons + ¼ cup)
Black pepper, freshly ground (1/2 tablespoon)
Cornstarch (1/2 teaspoon)
Garlic, minced (1 teaspoon)
Peanut oil (3 tablespoons)
Chili flakes (1/2 tablespoon) OR red pepper, crushed (1/2 tablespoon)
Brown sugar (2 tablespoons)
Water (1/3 cup)

Directions:

1. Set the oven at 450 degrees Fahrenheit to preheat. Meanwhile, fill a saucepan with water, cover, and heat to boiling.

2. Arrange the shrimp on a large baking tray, making sure they form an even layer. Bake in the oven for about ten minutes, flipping them over halfway through.

3. Fill the steamer basket with the frozen bao buns before placing over the saucepan containing the boiling water. Cook the buns for seven to ten minutes or until puffed and completely cooked. Set aside on a plate covered with a dampened towel.

4. Meanwhile, pour oil into a nonstick skillet. Heat on medium, then stir in the ginger and garlic. Once the ginger and garlic are sizzling, stir in the chili flakes and black pepper. Keep stirring as you pour in the sugar and soy sauce. Continue cooking for five minutes or until the sugar is completely dissolved in the spicy sauce.

5. Pour the cornstarch into a small bowl filled with water (1/4 cup). Stir to combine and then pour into the skillet mixture. Cook for about one to two minutes or until thickened. Set aside.

6. Once the shrimps are done, place them inside a large bowl filled with the spicy sauce. Toss to combine, making sure the shrimp is evenly coated.

7. Carefully open the steamed buns. Smear kewpie mayonnaise at the inner base of each bun and top with the shrimp. Serve garnished with shredded carrots and chopped green onions.

8. Enjoy.

Shrimp Tempura Filled Bao Buns with Sweet and Sour Sauce

Ingredients:

Buns:
Salt (1/4 teaspoon)
Sugar (1 teaspoon)
Water, warm (1/4 cup + ½ cup)
Coconut oil (1 tablespoon)
Yeast, active dry (1 tablespoon)
Flour, all purpose (1/4 cup + 1 ½ cups)
Sugar (2 tablespoons)
Baking powder (1/2 teaspoon)

Shrimp tempura:
Salt (1/4 teaspoon)
Ice water (1/3 cup)
White sugar (1/4 teaspoon)
Coconut oil – for frying
Egg yolk (1 piece)
Baking powder (1/2 teaspoon)
Rice wine (1/2 cup)
Shrimp, fresh, peeled, deveined (1/2 pound)
Flour, all purpose (1/4 cup)
Cornstarch (1/4 cup)
Salt (1/4 teaspoon)
Shortening (1 teaspoon)

Sweet and sour sauce:
Rice vinegar (1/3 cup)
Water (1 tablespoon)
Ketchup (3 tablespoons)
Cornstarch (1 tablespoon)
Pineapple juice (2/3 cup)
Sugar, light brown (1/3 cup)
Soy sauce (1 tablespoon)

Directions:

1. In a large bowl, pour the flour (1/4 cup), sugar (1 teaspoon), yeast, and warm water (1/4 cup). Whisk well to combine and set aside for thirty minutes to activate the yeast.

2. In a separate bowl, whisk the flour (1 ½ cups) together with the vegetable oil, warm water (1/2 cup), and sugar (2 tablespoons). Once well-blended, knead with floured hands until elastic and smooth. Meanwhile, coat the inside of a large bowl. Place the dough in it and cover with plastic wrap. Then, let the dough rise on the counter for about two hours and thirty minutes to three hours.

3. Once the dough is done rising, punch it down with your fist. Transfer the dough onto a surface that has been sprinkled with flour. Knead the

dough for five minutes before dividing it into 24 rounds. Arrange the dough balls on a flour-dusted baking sheet. Then, cover with plastic wrap and allow to rest for thirty minutes or until it becomes twice its size.

4. Transfer each of the dough balls onto a piece of wax paper. Place in the steamer and cook for about fifteen minutes or until nicely puffed. Transfer the steamed buns onto a platter and cover with a moistened towel.

5. Fill a medium bowl with the salt and rice wine. Stir to combine before adding in the shrimp. Toss until well-combined, and then place in the refrigerator to marinate for twenty to thirty minutes.

6. Fill a deep fryer with oil and then heat to 375 degrees Fahrenheit. Meanwhile, in a large bowl, whisk the all-purpose flour along with the cornstarch, baking powder, white sugar, salt, egg yolk, ice water, and shortening. Once well-blended, add the shrimp, one at a time, to coat on all sides.

7. Drop the coated shrimps in the hot oil and cook for one to two minutes or until golden brown. Transfer onto a plate lined with paper towels.

8. Heat a saucepan on medium. Add the rice vinegar, ketchup, pineapple juice, soy sauce, and brown sugar and stir to combine. Cook until boiling, then stir in the cornstarch slurry. Cook for another one to two minutes or until your sweet and sour sauce is thickened.

9. After opening the steamed buns, fill with the shrimp and drizzle with the sweet and sour sauce. Serve and enjoy right away.

Bao Buns with Crispy Fish Fillets

Ingredients:

Bao buns:
Baking powder (1/2 teaspoon)
Peanut oil (1 tablespoon + 1 tablespoon)
Caster sugar (a pinch)
Water (150 milliliters)
Flour, plain (2 cups)
Milk, warm (30 milliliters)
Yeast, dried (1 teaspoon)
Rice vinegar (3 teaspoons)

Fish fillets:
Flour, plain (1/4 cup)
Fish sauce (1 tablespoon + 1 teaspoon)
Coconut oil – for frying
Corn flour (1/2 cup)
Flathead fillets, boneless, skinless, sliced into 3 long portions (700 grams)
Garlic cloves, crushed (2 pieces)

Seasoning blend:
Coriander seeds (2 teaspoons)
Red chili, dried (1 piece)
Sichuan peppercorns (3 teaspoons)
Star anise (3 teaspoons)
Sea salt (3 tablespoons)

Slaw:
Chinese cabbage, shredded (3 cups)
Kewpie mayonnaise (1/2 cup)
Carrots, shredded (2 pieces)
Coriander leaves, chopped (1/3 cup)
Lime juice, freshly squeezed (2 teaspoons)

For serving:
Sriracha sauce
Coriander leaves
Lime slices

Directions:

1. In a large bowl, whisk the baking powder with the flour. In a smaller bowl, stir the yeast together with the caster sugar and milk. Once the yeast and sugar are completely dissolved, pour into the flour bowl. Pour in the rice vinegar, water, and oil as well, and give everything a good stir with a fork. Keep stirring until a soft dough forms, then place on a surface dusted lightly with flour. With floured hands, knead the dough for about ten minutes or until smooth.

2. Meanwhile, coat a large bowl with a little oil. Add the kneaded dough and cover with a towel, then allow the dough to rise for about one hour or until done with rising. Punch it down with your fist before cutting into 8 portions and shaping into small balls. Place the dough balls on a baking sheet dusted with flour, cover with plastic wrap or clean towel, and let sit for five minutes.

3. Use a rolling pin to shape each dough ball into a disk. After brushing with oil, fold across and set on top of a tray lined with baking paper. Cover with plastic wrap or towel and let sit for another twenty to thirty minutes or until done with their second rising. Meanwhile, line your bamboo steamer with baking paper. Add the buns and cook for about ten

minutes or until cooked through and nicely puffed. Set aside.

4. Dry-fry the peppercorns, star anise, and coriander in a large skillet heated on medium. Allow to cool before transferring into a mortar filled with salt and chili. Use a pestle to grind the ingredients together before adding to a large bowl. Add the flour and corn flour, whisking well to combine everything.

5. Fill a separate bowl with the garlic, fish sauce (1 tablespoon), and fish. Toss to combine before coating the fish with the seasoned flour mixture. Meanwhile, heat a large skillet on medium after pouring in the oil. After shaking any excess off the flour-coated fish, drop in the hot oil and fry until cooked through and golden. Place on a plate lined with paper towels and allow to drain and cool.

6. Mix the ingredients for the slaw in a medium bowl. Fill the steamed buns with divided portions of the slaw and top with the fried fish. Serve garnished with coriander, wedged lime, and sriracha.

Fish and Crab Bao Buns

Ingredients:

Buns:
Icing sugar (90 grams)
Yeast, instant dry (7 grams)
Baking powder (10 grams)
White vinegar (1/2 teaspoon)
Hong Kong flour (400 grams)
Butter (30 grams)
Water, cold (10 milliliters)
Water, lukewarm (160 milliliters)
Filling:
Otak-otak, frozen (100 grams)
Crabstick meat (6 pieces)
Luncheon meat, fried, sliced into cubes (50 grams)

Directions:

1. Sift the icing sugar and flour into a large bowl. Whisk to combine and then create a well at the center of the mixture. Pour the yeast, vinegar, and lukewarm water into the well. Stir to combine into a well-blended flour mixture. After adding the butter, knead the flour mixture for about ten to fifteen minutes or until you have a soft dough.

2. Dampen a cloth and place on top of the dough. Let it rise for thirty minutes or until puffed to twice its size.

3. Meanwhile, pour the baking powder into a small bowl filled with cold water. Stir to dissolve the baking powder before sprinkling all over the dough. Knead with floured hands, making sure the baking powder is incorporated into the dough. After cutting the dough into 16 pieces, roll into 3-inch circles. Fold each piece of dough before filling at the center with divided portions of the otak-otak, crabmeat, and luncheon meat. Gather the dough seams at the top and pinch to seal.

4. Place the filled buns in the steamer, making sure each has enough room to expand. Steam on high for twelve minutes or until cooked and puffed. Transfer onto a wire rack to keep the bottoms of the buns from getting soggy.

5. Serve and enjoy.

Salmon Teriyaki Bao Buns

Ingredients:

Buns:
Milk powder, skinned, dried (1 tablespoon)
Sea salt (1 pinch)
Yeast, fast action (1 teaspoon)
Coconut oil (1 tablespoon + 1 tablespoon)
Flour, plain (160 grams + ¼ cup for dusting)
Caster sugar (1 ½ tablespoons)
Baking powder (1 teaspoon)
Water, warm (90 milliliters)

Salmon:
Mirin (2 tablespoons)
Red chili, sliced into rounds (1 piece)
Tamari/soy sauce (2 tablespoons)
Honey, runny (2 tablespoons)
Salmon fillets, 5½-oz. (2 pieces)

For serving:
Lime, sliced into quarters (1 piece)
Spring onions, sliced diagonally into thin portions (4 pieces)
Coriander leaves, fresh (a handful)
Cucumber, small, sliced thinly into rounds (1 piece)

Directions:

1. Pour the chilli, honey, soy sauce, and mirin into a medium bowl. Stir to combine before adding the salmon fillets. Toss to coat the fish well, then cover and refrigerate.

2. Meanwhile, fill a large bowl with the bun dough's dry ingredients. Whisk well to combine, then create a well at the center of the mixture. Fill the well with the bun dough's wet ingredients and stir everything with a spoon. Once you have a well-blended mixture, knead for about two to three minutes or until the dough is elastic and smooth.

3. Transfer the dough into an oiled bowl. Use cling film to cover the dough. Let sit on the counter for forty-five minutes or until it rises to twice its size.

4. Make eight pieces of 4x4-inch squared of baking paper. Meanwhile, cover your work surface with a dusting of flour. Transfer the dough onto it and roll to form a sausage shape. Divide into 8 portions and mold into disks. Fold each across in half and place on a square of baking paper, then brush lightly with oil. Cover with cling film and allow to rise again for another thirty minutes.

5. Set the oven at 420 degrees Fahrenheit to preheat. Fill a baking dish with the salmon fillets. Bake in the oven for twenty minutes, making sure to cover the fillets with the marinade halfway. Once done, set the fillets on a plate and pour the remaining marinade into a small serving bowl.

6. Meanwhile, fill the steamer with the buns, including their paper covers at the bottom. Cook for about five to eight minutes or until you have these nicely puffed bao buns.

7. Carefully open the steamed bao buns and fill with the cooked salmon fillets, cucumber, lime, spring onions, and coriander. Serve with the dipping sauce (reserved marinade) and enjoy immediately.

Chile Butter Lobster Bao Buns

Ingredients:

Cilantro leaves, packed loosely (1 tablespoon)
Butter, unsalted, sliced into chunks (1/4 pound)
Lobster meat, cooked, sliced into chunks (10 ounces)
Red chile flakes (1/2 teaspoon)
Scallions, sliced thinly (1 tablespoon)
Bao buns, frozen/handmade, steamed (6 pieces)
Sriracha (1/4 cup)
Kosher salt (1/2 teaspoon + ¼ teaspoon for seasoning)
Lemon juice, freshly squeezed (1 tablespoon)

Directions:

1. Set the bao buns on a heat-proof plate. Cover with a damp cloth and heat in the microwave for one minute, flipping the buns halfway.

2. Heat a saucepan on medium-low. Add the butter and allow it to melt before stirring in the salt (1/2 teaspoon), chile flakes, and sriracha. Turn the heat down to low and stir in the lobster. Cook for one to two minutes or until the lobster meat is heated

through. Remove from heat and mix with the scallions, cilantro, and lemon juice.

3. Arrange the steamed buns on a plate after filling with lobster meat and sauce.

4. Serve immediately.

Bao Buns Stuffed with Fried Halibut

Ingredients:

Flour, all purpose (1/2 cup)
Breadcrumbs, panko (1 cup)
Halibut fillet, cut into 8 portions (1 pound)
Eggs (2 pieces)
Coconut oil – for frying

Pickled vegetables:
Rice wine vinegar (1/2 cup)
Red pepper, julienned (1/2 piece)
Salt (1 teaspoon)
Carrot, julienned (1 piece)
Celery stalk, julienned (1/2 piece)
Sugar (2 tablespoons)

Sauce:
Rice wine vinegar (1/4 cup)
Grapeseed oil (1/4 cup)
Korean chili sauce (1/4 cup)
Tamari soy sauce (1 teaspoon)

Directions:

1. Place all ingredients for the pickled vegetables in a medium bowl. Stir to combine and let sit for thirty minutes.

2. Pour all ingredients for the sauce into a small bowl and whisk well.

3. Place the buns in the steamer and cook for about eleven minutes or until cooked and puffed. Transfer onto a plate and keep warm with a damp towel.

4. Heat a skillet on medium after filling it with oil.

5. Coat each halibut fillet with flour before dipping in the eggs (whisked) and breadcrumbs. Add to the hot oil and cook on each side for two minutes. Transfer onto a plate and sprinkle with a little salt to taste.

6. Fill each steamed bun with the halibut and pickled vegetables. Serve with the sauce and enjoy.

Chapter 5. Appetizing Bao Buns with Meatless Filling

Coconut Filled Bao Buns

Ingredients:

Buns:
Bread flour, white (1 1/8 cups)
Sugar (1/2 teaspoon)
Coconut oil (1 ½ tablespoons)
Sugar (1/6 cup)
Egg, large, fork-beaten (1/2 piece)
Water, warm (1/6 cup)
Yeast, active dry (1 teaspoon)
Salt (1/4 teaspoon)
Water, boiling (1/8 cup)

Filling:
Sugar, granulated (1 tablespoon)
Egg yolk, large (1 piece)
Coconut flakes (1 1/3 cups)
Butter, melted (2 tablespoons)

Egg wash:
Water (1 tablespoon)
Egg, large (1 piece)

Honey wash:
Water (1 tablespoon)
Honey, liquid (1 tablespoon)

Directions:

1. Fill the blender with the sugar and coconut. Process until blended into a fine mixture and pour into a medium bowl. Add the egg yolk and melted butter and stir to combine into a paste. Set aside the filling.

2. Fill a small dish with sugar (1/2 portion) and warm water. Stir to dissolve the sugar before sprinkling the yeast on top of the mixture. Stir to combine, then let sit for ten minutes or until the yeast is activated.

3. Fill a large bowl with the remaining sugar (1/2 portion), cooking oil, and salt. Stir continuously as you add the boiling water and let the sugar dissolve completely. Add the yeast mixture and egg and stir until well-combined. Add the flour and stir until you have a soft dough. Transfer the dough onto your flour-dusted work surface. Knead for ten minutes or until elastic and smooth, then place inside a greased bowl. Cover with plastic wrap and

kitchen towel before setting on the counter. Let the dough rise for one hour and thirty minutes.

4. Once the dough has doubled in size, knock it down and cover again with plastic wrap and kitchen towel. After five minutes, return to the floured surface and roll into a 12-inch-long log. Slice into 6 equal sized portions.

5. Fill each bun with the filling. After sealing up all the buns, place on a baking sheet and cover with plastic wrap and kitchen towel. Let the buns rest for one hour or until they expand to twice their size.

6. Use a fork to combine the water and egg. Brush the egg wash over the filled buns before placing in the steamer. Cook for fifteen to eighteen minutes or until cooked through and fluffy.

7. Mix the hot water with the honey before brushing all over the bao buns. Serve immediately.

Pulled Jackfruit Bao Buns

Ingredients:

Buns:
Sea salt, fine (1 teaspoon)
Yeast, instant active (2 teaspoons)
Bao flour (2 ½ cups) OR all-purpose flour (2 ½ cups)
Coconut oil (1 ½ tablespoons)
Sugar (2 teaspoons)

Filling:
Coconut oil (2 tablespoons) – for frying
Spring onions, small, sliced (2 pieces)
Rice vinegar (1 tablespoon)
Garlic cloves, chopped finely (3 pieces)
Maple syrup/brown sugar (2 teaspoons)
Jackfruit, green/young (560 grams)
Ginger, grated (4 teaspoons)
Tamari/soy sauce (3 teaspoons)
Hoisin sauce (2 tablespoons + 2 tablespoon for serving)
Chinese 5-spice (1 teaspoon)

Condiments:
Red cabbage, finely shredded (1 cup)
English cucumber, julienned (1/2 piece)
Spring onion, finely sliced (2 tablespoons)
Chili sauce (1/4 teaspoon) OR chili, fresh, sliced (1/4 teaspoon)
Turnip, julienned (1 piece) OR daikon, julienned (1/2 piece)
Peanuts, unsalted, roasted, chopped/crushed (a handful)
Coriander, fresh, chopped (a handful)

Directions:

1. Fill a large bowl with the flour, sugar, salt, and instant yeast. Whisk to combine before adding the warm water (1/2 cup) and oil (1 ½ tablespoons). Using a wooden spoon, whisk until roughly blended into a dough. Knead with floured hands for ten minutes or until the dough turns out smooth and elastic. Mold the dough into a bowl before lightly coating with oil. Place in a large bowl and cover with a towel. Place somewhere warm for one to two hours so the dough can rise to twice its size.

2. Line the bamboo steamer with baking paper. Meanwhile, cut out 8 squares from a sheet of baking paper.

3. Once done rising, transfer the dough onto a floured surface. Knock down with your fist before cutting into 8 pieces. Shape into balls and allow to rest, covered, for thirty minutes.

4. Mold the dough balls into ovals before folding across in half and lining the inside with the baking paper squares. Add the buns to the lined steamer and let sit for thirty minutes.

5. Steam the buns for ten minutes. Remove from heat and let the buns rest for five minutes inside the steamer before transferring onto a plate covered with damp towel.

6. Meanwhile, heat a large skillet on medium. Add oil (2 tablespoons); once hot, stir in the spring onions. Once the spring onions are softened, stir in the ginger and chopped garlic and cook until fragrant. Stir in the five spice and cook for one minute before pouring in the remaining filling ingredients. Stir to combine as well as dissolve the sugar. Stir in the jackfruit and cook for another five minutes or until the entire mixture is reduced.

7. Open each steamed bun and fill with divided portions of the jackfruit mixture. Add the condiments and serve right away.

Bao Buns with Custard Filling

Ingredients:

Bao Buns:
Water, cold (4 ½ teaspoons)
Water, warm (1/4 cup)
Milk, whole, warm (1 cup)
Flour, all purpose (4 cups)
Baking powder (1 tablespoon)
Sugar, granulated (1/2 cup + 1 tablespoon)
Active dry yeast (2 ¼ teaspoons)
Vegetable shortening (2 tablespoons)
Coconut oil (1 tablespoon)

Custard filling:
Egg yolks, large (5 pieces)
Heavy cream (1/2 cup)
Butter, unsalted, sliced into 4 equal portions (1/4 cup)
Milk, whole (1 ½ cups)
Sugar, granulated (1/2 cup)
Cornstarch (1/4 cup)
Vanilla extract, pure (1 ½ teaspoons)

Directions:

1. Fill a large saucepan with the cream and milk. Stir to combine and heat on medium. Once the mixture is simmering, add the sugar (1/4 cup) and whisk well. Remove from heat once the sugar is completely dissolved.

2. Place the egg yolks in a large bowl and whisk well. Add the sugar (1/4 cup) and whisk again until well-combined and smooth. Pour in the cornstarch and whisk until everything is evenly blended.

3. Meanwhile, take a quarter of a cup of the slightly cooled milk mixture and stream into the egg yolk mixture. Whisk well to temper, then pour the tempered egg yolk mixture into the rest of the milk mixture as you keep on whisking. Heat on medium-high and, whisking continuously, allow the entire mixture to cook for three minutes or until thickened. Remove from heat before mixing in the vanilla and cold butter. Cover with cling film and allow to chill in the refrigerator for two to three hours.

4. Fill a deep dish with the yeast, sugar, and warm water. Set aside for two to three minutes before stirring to combine. Set aside again for ten minutes or until foaming.

5. Sift the flour into a large bowl, then create a well in its center. Meanwhile, combine the yeast mixture with the shortening, milk, and sugar in another bowl. Once the shortening is partially dissolved, pour the wet mixture into the well in the flour. Mix everything into a smooth dough.

6. Sprinkle a little flour all over your work surface. Place the dough on the surface and knead for about ten minutes or until elastic and smooth. Lightly brush all sides of the dough with oil before placing in a bowl and covering with cling film and a clean towel. Set on the kitchen counter for one hour and thirty minutes to let the dough rise to twice its size.

7. Once the dough is done rising to the desired size, knock it down and return to the floured surface. Roll it out into a ¾-inch-thick rectangle. Meanwhile, stir the baking powder into a small bowl filled with cold water. Brush the mixture all over the dough before kneading for ten minutes or until the dough feels smoother and firmer. Return to the bowl and cover again with cling wrap and a towel. Let the dough rest for half an hour.

8. Transfer the dough onto the floured surface and cut into 24 even-sized portions. Roll each piece of dough into a ball, then flatten with your palm to

form a disk that is thick at the center and thinned out on the edges.

9. Place the filling (1 tablespoon) in the middle of each dough disk. Form each filled dough piece into a bun. Place all filled buns on a parchment-lined baking sheet to rest, covered, for thirty minutes.

10. Fill the bottom of the steamer with enough water to make it one-inch-deep, making sure the water is not in direct contact with the steamer insert's bottom side. Cover and allow the water to boil before adding the buns (do this in batches). Cover and cook on medium-high for about five to six minutes or until puffed and cooked.

11. Serve hot.

Bao Buns Stuffed with Greens

Ingredients:

Buns:
Honey (1 tablespoon)
All-purpose flour (3 ½ cups)
Milk, soy/almond, plain, at room temp. (1 cup)
Water, warm (1/2 cup)
Yeast, active dry (2 ¼ teaspoons)
Salt (1/2 teaspoon)

Greens:
Pepper, freshly ground (1/4 teaspoon)
Salt (1/4 teaspoon)
Olive oil, extra virgin (1/4 cup)
Bok choy, sliced into half-inch pieces (1/2 pound)
Sweet chile sauce (2 tablespoons)
Garlic cloves, minced (6 pieces)
Soy sauce (2 tablespoons)
Mustard greens/kale, trimmed (1/2 pound)
Shiitake mushrooms, w/ stems removed, w/ caps sliced thinly (10 ounces)
Shallots, large, minced (2 pieces)
Basil, chopped (1/2 cup)
Sriracha, divided (1/2 teaspoon) – for serving

Directions:

1. Pour the honey and warm water into a large bowl. Sprinkle the yeast on top, then whisk to combine. Let the yeast mixture sit for ten minutes or until foamy; set aside.

2. Pour the flour and salt into a separate bowl. Meanwhile, add the almond milk to the activated yeast mixture. Stir to combine before pouring into the flour bowl. Stir continuously until you have a well-blended mixture, then knead until smooth and a bit sticky. Place the dough inside a large bowl greased with a bit of oil and cover with plastic wrap. Then, let it sit on your counter for fifty minutes or until doubled in size.

3. Fill a medium saucepan with salted water and heat on medium. Once boiling, add the greens and cook for one minute to tenderize. After draining well, allow the greens to cool. Squeeze them dry before chopping coarsely into bits. Set aside.

4. Meanwhile, heat a large skillet on medium before pouring in the olive oil (3 tablespoons). Once hot, stir in the mushrooms and cook for four minutes or until softened. Pour in the shallots, remaining olive oil (1 tablespoon), and garlic; stir continuously as the mushroom mixture cooks for

three minutes or until tender. Stir in the bok choy before covering the skillet to allow the filling to cook for five minutes or until tender. Before removing from heat, stir in the soy sauce, sweet chile sauce, chives, basil, and greens. Add pepper and salt to taste and set aside to cool.

5. Make 16 paper squares (3 ½-inch) from a piece of parchment. Meanwhile, knock down the dough before transferring to a surface that has been dusted with flour. Form 16 equal sized balls out of the dough, then shape each piece of dough into a circle. Arrange the dough balls on a parchment lined sheet and dust with flour. Cover with cling film before letting them rest for ten minutes.

6. After ten minutes, top each piece of dough with the filling (3 tablespoons). Seal each bun by pinching at the seams and place on a parchment square. Arrange all parchment-lined buns in the steamer. Cook on medium-high for ten minutes or until you have firm and cooked through bao buns.

7. Serve right away.

Easy Red Bean Bao Buns

Ingredients:

Butter (1 tablespoon)
Yeast, instant (1 ½ teaspoons)
Red bean paste (6 ounces)
Milk (1/2 cup)
Water, lukewarm (1/2 cup)
Baking powder (1/2 teaspoon)
Flour, unbleached (3 cups)
Sugar (1/4 cup)

Directions:

1. Fill a large bowl with the flour, baking powder, sugar, butter, and milk. Whisk well to combine.

2. Stir the yeast into the lukewarm water. Once well-mixed, pour into the flour mixture. Stir until everything is well-blended into a doughy texture. With floured hands, knead the dough for ten to twelve minutes or until smooth and stretchy.

3. Gather the dough into a ball and place at the bottom of an oiled bowl. Cover with cling film before letting the dough sit for one hour to rise.

4. Once the dough is doubled in size, turn it out onto a surface prepped with a little flour. Cut the dough into 12 portions. Set aside for two minutes, then flatten each piece of dough into a disk.

5. Top the center of each bun with filling (1 tablespoon). Twist the buns at the corners to secure their fillings before placing on parchment paper squares.

6. Arrange all filled bao buns in the steamer. Cook for about fifteen minutes or until you have white, shiny, and firm bao buns.

7. Serve and enjoy right away. .

Shiitake Bok Choy Bao Buns

Ingredients:

Bao buns:
Yeast, instant (1 teaspoon)
Cornstarch (2 tablespoons)
Coconut oil (1 tablespoon + 1 teaspoon)
Baking soda (1/8 teaspoon)
Water, warm (3/4 cup)
Sugar, granulated (1 tablespoon)
Flour, all purpose (2 cups)
Salt (1/4 teaspoon)

Shiitake bok choy:
Salt (1/2 teaspoon)
Shiitake mushrooms, fresh, large (8 pieces)
Sugar (1/2 teaspoon)
Bean curd, dried (4 ounces)
White pepper, freshly ground (1/8 teaspoon)
Baby bok choy, thoroughly washed (1 pound)
Coconut oil, divided (3 tablespoons)
Soy sauce, light (1 teaspoon)
Sesame oil (1/2 tablespoon)

Directions:

1. Heat a pot filled with water on medium-high. Meanwhile, prepare an ice bath and set aside.

2. Once the water in the pot is on a rolling boil, add the bok choy in 2 batches and blanch for ten seconds each time. Quickly drop the blanched bok choy into the prepared ice bath. Once completely cooled, strain and squeeze to dry, chop and set aside in a bowl.

3. After chopping the mushrooms into fine bits, add to a large nonstick skillet filled with oil (2 tablespoons) and heated on medium. Stir and cook for three to four minutes or until softened. Set aside to cool.

4. Meanwhile, add the dried bean curd to a food processor and chop finely. Discard any liquid from the bowl with the chopped bok choy before pouring in the dried bean curd. Add the cooked mushrooms as well as the soy sauce, sesame oil, oil (1 tablespoon), white pepper, sugar, and salt to taste. Stir to combine, then set aside in the refrigerator.

5. Fill a small bowl with the yeast, sugar, and water. Whisk until the yeast is completely dissolved. Set aside for fifteen minutes so that the yeast can

bloom. Once the yeast mixture is foaming, stir in oil (1 tablespoon).

6. Place the flour in a large bowl. Add the baking soda, cornstarch, and salt and whisk well. With a spatula, stir the yeast mixture into the flour mixture. Once everything is well-combined into a soft dough, use your floured hands to knead the dough until smooth and elastic without being sticky (adding flour by the spoonful can help achieve this).

7. After brushing the surface of the dough with oil (1 teaspoon), place in a bowl and cover with cling film. Set aside on the counter to rest for one hour or until puffed to twice its size. Knock the risen dough with your fist before kneading for two to three minutes. Cut the dough into 14 equal sized rounds, arrange on a parchment paper lined baking sheet, and cover with a tea towel. Set aside.

8. Meanwhile, make 14 parchment paper squares (3x3-inch) for lining the bao buns.

9. Dust your work surface with flour before turning out the dough balls onto it. Shape each dough round into a 4-inch-diameter ball, then flatten into a thick-centered disk. Onto the center of each bun, place the filling (2 ½ tablespoons). Seal at the top

before letting sit on a square of parchment. Arrange all filled buns inside the steamer and cook for twenty minutes or until completely cooked.

10. Serve and enjoy.

Breakfast Bao Buns

Ingredients:

Bao buns, steamed (2 pieces)
Cucumber slices (8 pieces)
Sriracha (1/2 teaspoon)
Egg, lightly beaten (1 piece)
Hoisin sauce (1/2 teaspoon)
Green onions (1 teaspoon)

Directions:

1. Heat a nonstick skillet over medium-low heat before adding a little oil to coat at the bottom. Once hot, pour a small portion of the beaten egg and swirl to form an even, crepe-like layer. Reduce heat to low and leave the egg alone to cook for fifteen seconds, then flip onto its other side to cook for another fifteen seconds. Transfer onto a plate and fold to form a square. Repeat until all the egg is used up. Add pepper and salt to taste and set aside.

2. Meanwhile, arrange the buns on a heat-proof plate. Use a dampened paper towel to cover the buns and heat in the microwave for one minute. Cover each bun with hoisin sauce at the bottom

before filling inside with a piece of folded crepe-y egg.

3. Serve your breakfast bao buns hot and garnished with cucumber slices, green onions, and sriracha.

Tofu Bao Buns with Cucumber Salad

Ingredients:

Bao buns:
Coconut oil (1 tablespoon)
Caster sugar (1 teaspoon)
Flour, plain (220 grams + 4 tablespoons)
Water, warm (4 tablespoons + ½ cup)
Caster sugar (2 tablespoons)
Baking yeast, dried active (1 tablespoon)
Salt (1/4 teaspoon)
Baking powder (1/2 teaspoon)

Tofu:
Peppercorns, 5-blend, freshly ground (1 ½ tablespoons)
Cilantro leaves, rinsed, dried, chopped coarsely (3 tablespoons)
Tofu, firm, pressed overnight (16 ounces)
Potato starch (4 tablespoons)
Sesame seeds, toasted (1 teaspoon)
Garlic, minced (2 teaspoons)
Ginger, fresh, 1-inch, peeled, julienned (1 piece) OR ginger, minced (4 teaspoons)
Scallions, julienned (4 pieces)
Peppercorns, Szechwan, freshly ground (1/2 tablespoon)

Sea salt (2 teaspoons)
Coconut oil – for frying

Cucumber salad:
Rice vinegar (2 tablespoons)
Sea salt (1/2 teaspoon)
Chili flakes, dried (1/4 teaspoon)
English cucumbers, sliced thinly into rounds (1 ½ pieces) OR Persian cucumbers, sliced thinly into rounds (3 pieces)
Cane sugar, raw (3/4 teaspoon)
Sesame oil, toasted (1/2 tablespoon)
Cilantro leaves, rinsed, dried, chopped coarsely (1/2 teaspoon)

Peanut topping:
Cane sugar, raw (2 ½ tablespoons)
Peanuts, unsalted, roasted (1/2 cup)

Directions:

1. In a large bowl, toss the cucumber slices with salt and let stand for half an hour. Drain well after rinsing. Meanwhile, toss the dried chili flakes with the toasted sesame oil, rice vinegar, and sugar. Pour this mixture into the cucumber bowl, along

with the cilantro. Toss to combine and place in the refrigerator for one hour.

2. Place the peanuts in a mortar and crush with a pestle until coarsely chopped. Mix with sugar before setting aside in an airtight jar.

3. Wipe clean the mortar and fill with the Szechwan peppercorns. Grind with a pestle and set aside in a small bowl. Repeat with the 5-blend peppercorns.

4. Fill a baking dish with the ground Szechwan peppercorns (1/2 tablespoon), ground 5-blend peppercorns (1 ½ tablespoons), salt, and potato starch. Stir to combine and spread to form an even layer at the bottom of the baking dish. Cut the tofu into 10 portions before adding to the mixture and toss until the tofu blocks are well-coated.

5. Heat a large wok on medium before adding the coconut oil. Once the oil is hot, add the coated tofu pieces in batches. Add the scallions, garlic, and ginger and stir-fry for about four to five minutes or until lightly browned. Sprinkle sesame seeds all over the cooked tofu and set aside.

6. Stir the yeast, flour (4 tablespoons), sugar (1 teaspoon), and warm water (4 tablespoons) together in a small bowl. Add the rest of the flour,

sugar, and warm water, along with the salt and coconut oil and mix well into a dough. Knead the dough with floured hands; once smooth and stretchy, transfer into an oiled bowl and place on the counter. Allow the dough to rise for two hours and thirty minutes to three hours or until proven.

7. Knock down the dough before spreading out onto a floured surface. Dust its surface with baking powder and knead for five minutes. Cut into 12 portions and roll each into a ball. Place each dough ball on a piece of parchment. Cover all the buns with cling wrap and a kitchen towel and allow to rise for another half hour.

8. Once the buns are done rising, place inside the steamer and cook for ten minutes or until cooked through and nicely puffed. Fill with the tofu, cucumber salad, peanuts, scallions, and cilantro.

9. Serve and enjoy right away.

Oyster Mushroom and Seitan Bao Buns

Ingredients:

Bao buns:
Water, warmed to 110 degrees Fahrenheit (2 tablespoons + ¾ cups)
Sugar (2 teaspoons)
Flour (2 ¼ cups)
Instant yeast (2 ¼ teaspoons)

Seitan:
Wheat gluten (3/4 cup)
Brown sugar (1 ½ tablespoons)
Chinese 5-spice (1/4 teaspoon)
Shaoxing wine (2 teaspoons)
Water (1/4 cup)
Garlic cloves, crushed (4 pieces)
Soy sauce, light (1 tablespoon)
Bouillon powder, mushroom (1 teaspoon)
Sesame oil (1/2 teaspoon)

Sauce:
Ginger, 1-inch diameter, ¼-inch thick (1 slice)
Oyster mushroom, diced (1 cup)
Soy sauce, light (1 teaspoon)
Maltose/corn syrup (2 tablespoons)
Chinese 5-spice (1/4 teaspoon)

Coconut oil (2 teaspoons)
Hoisin sauce (1/4 cup)
Shaoxing wine (1 tablespoon)
Soy sauce, dark (1 teaspoon)
Red onion/shallot, diced (1/2 cup)

Slurry:
Flour (2 tablespoons)
Water (1/2 cup)
Bouillon powder, mushroom (1/2 teaspoon)

Directions:

1. Place all of the ingredients for the seitan (except the wheat gluten) in a medium bowl. Whisk to combine, then add the gluten. Whisk again to form a doughy mixture, then knead gently with floured hands. Cover tightly with parchment paper and cook in the steamer for forty-five minutes or until completely cooked. Once done, allow to cool on a rack for five to ten minutes. Transfer in the refrigerator and allow it to chill and firm up before chopping into half-inch chunks. Set aside.

2. Meanwhile, place all the ingredients for the dough in a large bowl. Whisk well to combine into sticky dough, then knead with floured hands for about five to ten minutes or until smooth and

elastic. Place the dough in a bowl greased with oil, cover with a damp and moist towel, and set on the counter for one hour or until the dough is doubled in size.

3. Place the ingredients for the slurry in a small bowl. Stir to combine and set aside.

4. Heat a large skillet on medium-high after filling it with oil (2 teaspoons). Once the oil is hot, stir in the ginger and cook for one minute or until lightly browned. Stir in the onion and cook for three minutes or until softened, then reduce heat to medium and stir in the mushrooms. Cook for five minutes or until the mushrooms have softened before stirring in the five spice powder, soy sauce, maltose/corn syrup, shaoxing wine, and hoisin sauce. Let the mixture cook for another two to three minutes or until bubbling. Gently stream in the slurry as you stir the mixture continuously. Let it cook for another one minute to thicken. Stir the seitan chunks, then allow the entire mixture to chill before serving.

5. Meanwhile, place the dough on a surface dusted with flour. Knead with floured hands for a few minutes before shaping into a log. Cut the dough into 12 equal portions, then roll into half-inch-thick

balls, with the center being much thicker than the edges.

6. Remove the ginger from the filling before placing one tablespoon into each bun. Place each filled bun on top of a muffin liner and then place on a large baking tray. Cover with a kitchen towel and allow for a second rising.

7. After thirty minutes (or once the buns are doubled in size), place them inside a steamer basket set over a large pot that has been heated on high and filled with boiling water. Cook the buns for ten minutes or until puffed and firm. Remove from heat and let the steamed buns rest in the steamer for two to five minutes, before transferring the buns onto a platter.

8. Serve and enjoy.

Kimchi Bao Buns

Ingredients:

Buns:
Milk, lukewarm (1/4 cup)
Yeast (1 teaspoon)
Salt (3/4 teaspoon)
Milk, nonfat, dried (1 ½ tablespoons)
Water, lukewarm (1/3 cup)
Flour, all purpose, unbleached (1 ¾ cups)
Potato starch (1 tablespoon)
Sugar (1 tablespoon)
Butter, unsalted, soft (2 tablespoons)
Kimchi, chopped (1 cup)

Sauce:
Sesame oil, toasted (2 tablespoons)
Cilantro, chopped (a handful)
Tamari/soy sauce (1/2 cup)
Chili oil (a drop)
Curry powder (1/4 teaspoon)

Directions:

1. Fill the bowl of your stand mixer with the flour, potato starch, yeast, sugar, butter, milk, and water. Beat on low speed for one to two minutes or until well-mixed before sprinkling in the salt. Switch to medium speed as you beat the mixture while sprinkling in the salt. Keep kneading until you have a smooth dough.

2. Grease the inside of a large bowl with a little oil. Place the dough inside and cover with a kitchen towel. Allow the dough to rise for one hour. Knock down the dough before slicing into 8 portions.

3. Grease a cake pan (8x8) with a little oil; set aside. Meanwhile, place the kimchi on a plate lined with paper towels so any excess liquid can drain out.

4. With floured hands, mold each piece of dough into a big ravioli shape, making sure each piece is thick at the center and thin around the edges. Fill the center of each dough piece with the kimchi (1 tablespoon) before reshaping into a sealed bun. Arrange the filled buns at the bottom of the greased cake pan, then cover with cling wrap. Let the buns rise for one hour.

5. Line the bamboo steamer with parchment squares. Top with the buns and set over a pot filled with simmering water. Allow the buns to get steamed for twenty-five minutes or until cooked though.

6. Whisk the curry powder, tamari/soy sauce, toasted sesame oil, chili oil, and chopped cilantro together. Serve with the hot buns and enjoy right away.

Kimchi and Avocado Mayo Tofu Bao Buns

Ingredients:

Tofu slices, extra firm, dried, cut into half-inch cubes (3 pieces)
Kimchi paste (1/2 tablespoon)
Five spice blend (1/2 teaspoon)
Red onions, pickled (1 tablespoon)
Bao buns, steamed (3 pieces)
Cornstarch (1 tablespoon)
Mayonnaise (1 tablespoon)
Avocado, sliced (1/2 piece)

Directions:

1. Press the tofu until most of its liquid is drawn out.

2. In a large bowl, stir the cornstarch, salt, and five spice seasoning together until well-mixed. Add the tofu and toss until evenly coated.

3. Heat a large skillet on medium-high before pouring in the oil. Once the oil's temperature reaches 370 degrees Fahrenheit, add the seasoned tofu and fry until golden brown and cooked through. Allow the cooked tofu pieces to drain

excess oil on a plated lined with paper towels. Season with a sprinkling of salt.

4. Place the buns in the steamer and cook until nicely puffed and cooked through. Set aside on a plate and keep warm by covering with a damp cloth.

5. Meanwhile, stir the kimchi paste and mayonnaise together. Spread this mixture at the inner base of each steamed bun.

6. Fill each bun with equal portions of the tofu, avocado, and picked red onion.

7. Serve immediately.

Orange Sesame Tofu Bao Buns

Ingredients:

Sesame seeds, toasted (1 tablespoon)
Soy sauce (1 tablespoon)
Tofu slices, 1-inch, extra firm, pressed, dried (3 pieces)
Rice wine vinegar (1 teaspoon)
Sriracha (1 squirt)
Bao buns, frozen, steamed (3 pieces)
Cornstarch (1 tablespoon)
Orange marmalade (3 tablespoons)
Sesame oil (2 to 3 dashes)
Basil leaves (9 pieces)
Coconut oil – for frying

Directions:

1. Fill a small saucepan with the orange marmalade. Add the rice wine vinegar, sesame oil, sriracha, and soy sauce. Whisk well to combine before heating on medium-high. Stirring continuously, cook the mixture until bubbling and reduced to a thick sauce. Set aside in a large bowl.

2. Place the cornstarch in a medium bowl. Add the tofu and gently toss to coat the tofu on all sides.

Meanwhile, heat a large nonstick skillet on medium-high before pouring in the oil. Once heated through, drop the coated tofu and cook until crisp and golden.

3. Transfer the tofu nuggets in the bowl with the prepared sauce. Toss until well-combined, then set aside.

4. Meanwhile, carefully open the steamed buns. Place divided portions of the tofu nuggets inside each bun and then sprinkle with toasted sesame seeds and fresh basil.

5. Serve and enjoy.

Conclusion

Thank you again for purchasing this book!

I hope this book was able to help you to discover the joy of making – and eating – bao buns, of being bold enough to take the big leap from preparing your usual comfort foods to whipping up these flavor-packed, steamed creations.

The next step is to explore new ingredients and come up with your own new recipes, all designed to whet your appetite and satisfy your hunger. With this book by your side, a quick meal or snack will never be boring again.

Finally, if you enjoyed this book, please take the time to share your thoughts and post a review on Amazon. It'd be greatly appreciated!

Thank you and good luck!

Made in the USA
Middletown, DE
12 January 2020